Relax. Kids Can Organize. Parents too!

Growing Up Organized: A Mom-to-Mom Guide©

By Professional Organizer Lea Schneider

To Dear Lou, Don't worry. If anything happens, I've got the attic (fridge) covered. Love Lea

Dedicated with love to
Troy, Ashley and Nikki,
who taught me everything.

Are you crazed by clutter?

Frustrated because the kids can't find their things?

Does just trying to get out the door drive you mad?

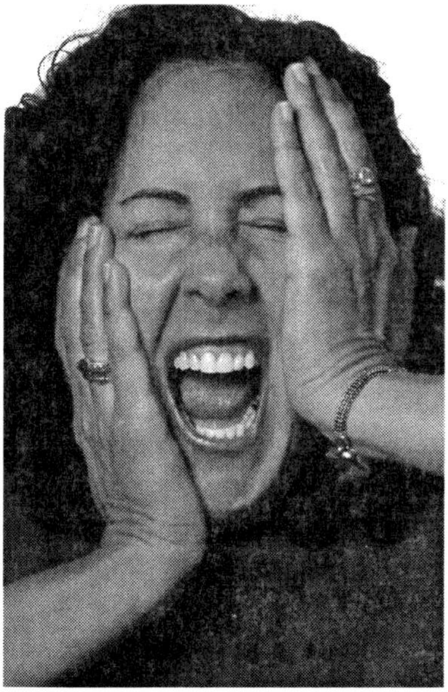

Relax.

Kids Can Organize. Parents too!

Growing Up Organized: A Mom-to-Mom Guide©

By Professional Organizer Lea Schneider

Index

Growing Up Organized: A Mom-to-Mom Guide©

By Professional Organizer Lea Schneider

"I can't be funny," I moaned, shaking my head for about the millionth time over the start of this book.

Lowering the ever-present newspaper from his face, my husband peered over his glasses and said "What do you mean you can't be funny? Are you always funny?"

Well, of course I am not always funny I explained, but there is some sort of rule about public speaking and even about writing. The basic rule is to start off funny.

"I know why the proverbial chicken crossed the road," I might tell a room full of women, as I give them a speech on organizing. "She thinks her keys might be over there somewhere."

"You know you're disorganized if," I intone to a group of laughing and nodding young mothers, taking a cue from comedian Jeff Foxworthy. "You're riding in the car and your child pipes up and says "Momma, where's the baby?"

Sure I laugh along with them, just to keep from crying!

I remember forgetting the baby. I remember losing the keys. Well, okay the keys were just last month and were more like a family comedy of errors, but the baby wasn't funny.

You know you are disorganized if.... You are riding in the car and your child pipes up and asks "Momma, where's the baby?"

With a husband on the road covering NFL football, I wasn't a single working mom but I was a working mom home alone with tykes. One exhausting Saturday, my two-year old dawdled as she sat strapped in her bight yellow highchair. She was enjoying creating works of art in the tomato sauce of the SpaghettiO's® and shouting "no" when I tried to clean her up. Giving up for a moment, I cleaned up the four year-old's face and hands and stepped around the corner to his room to tuck him in for a nap.

The next thing I know, I awoke with a start, my wrinkled cheek stuck to his cars and trunks comforter, wondering where I was. My son slumbered peacefully with his Cholly Dolly tucked under his arm. My next thought was the normal mother thought on waking – happens every time, every day- you're mentally taking inventory of what is going on with the children. Immediately, I was struck with a stab of fear.

"Where's the baby,"

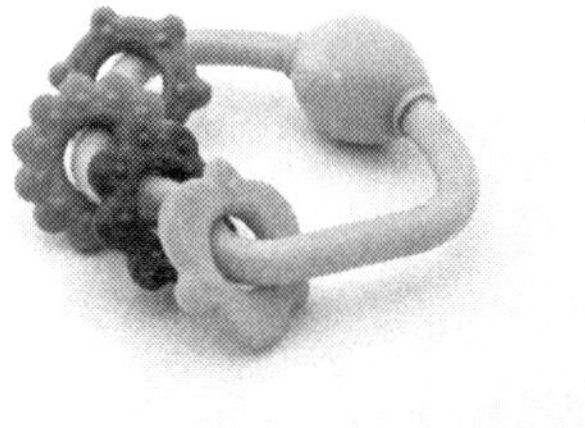

I thought, leaping up and racing in to her crib, which I found empty. Down the hall, a peek at toys here and there but no baby in sight. Around the corner and into the kitchen, and there she was. Sound asleep, slumped down in the high chair, held securely by the safety strap. The SpaghettiO's® had dried on her face and the top of her snow-white hair and glued themselves to the high chair tray.

I collapsed into a chair and burst into tears.

So I may joke about losing the baby but that is because I have been there and done that. In real life, this kind of chaos is just not funny.

No doubt you want your life to become more organized and you want your household to run more smoothly.

Well, what are you waiting for?

Are you waiting for summer to be over? For the eight-year-old to go to college? To have less stuff? To have more time?

We are waiting and not doing. That is the problem.

Looking back, I know that in my early years of motherhood, I was led by some misguided dream that things would get better, calmer, more organized – a miracle perhaps? One can always hope.

If only my husband wasn't always on the road, I'd ponder, blaming the travel.

By the time, I got my wish and he stopped traveling, I had three young children and he worked nights. What I remember most from those days is nursing the baby on the soccer field, trying not to yell "run" in her little ear as the five-year old kicked the ball and keeping one eye peeled on the three-year old climbing the playground equipment.

One night, holding baby to breast with one arm and a wet tissue to a skinned knee with the other hand, as I attempted to be a cheerleader for the soccer star, I started to panic. I

knew when I got home that I would have dinner to prepare and lunch boxes to clean up, spelling words to do, lunches to pack, a diaper bag to pack and clutter and papers to corral. I just wanted to crawl into bed. Thankfully, my night-working hubby was good about daytime laundry and vacuum running. That night, I sat at the field and daydreamed that when they were all potty trained and in school, things would get easier.

Of course, little did I know about educational systems at that point! I had no idea the darlings would end up in three different schools so that I always had to be in three places at once. Racing in the door from work and back out with t-ball equipment, Cub Scout derby cars or Halloween costumes, I imagined days would get easier when Dad doesn't work nights and can help out more by splitting the kids' activities with me.

By the time that wish came true, and Dad worked days, we were only busier as all three were old enough to participate in sports and activities in addition to school. The number three was part of the problem. We were only prepared for 'man to man defense' as my sportswriter husband used to joke when instead, we needed a zone defense plan.

Somewhere along this journey, I remember talking to my husband at the height of a day's particular crisis. Just how, oh how, was I going to get everything done?

"I just want things to be normal around here," I wailed.

"Honey," he said, putting his arms around me, "This is normal."

That was the straw that broke the camel's back. After a good cry, mumbling things better not printed, I figured out that if this was normal family life, something was going to change.

I did finally get those kids into one school but life did not get simpler. Family life became simpler because I learned to transfer many of my organizing skills on the job to my home.

By this time, my two highschoolers, who I chauffeured, played four varsity sports each – golf, football, boys' basketball, boys' soccer, volleyball, girls' basketball, girls' soccer and track.

Did I mention I worked full-time?

The middle school daughter played tennis and was a cheerleader- meaning adding the middle school basketball and football games to the calendar. Let's not forget practices. Then there were clubs and church group, activities with friends and let's not forget my own career ambitions! At the time all this was going on, one child was working at a greenhouse, one hostessing at a restaurant and one working in the church nursery. Oh, and did I mention the plays and musicals they enjoyed so much?

How about the basketball musical daughter? I used to fill a plate with dinner, drive to school and meet her at the gym door. She would eat it in the car as we drove to the other send of the long building where she would hop out and on stage to dance, with the coach telling my tall child to "play big" and the musical director telling her to be duck down to blend in.

I am not sure how I had time to go to work!

Here is some of what I learned along the way.

No matter what you do you are limited to 24 hours. To stay healthy, you have to sleep eight hours. Now you have 16 hours left. If you have a job you spend eight at work, one at lunch and one-half commuting. You have six and a half left.

You spend an hour getting yourself and children ready in the morning.

You spend an hour winding down and getting prepared in the evening.

You are now down to 4.5 hours. You have 4.5 hours to cook, clean, pay bills, help with homework, get laundry done, go to the store, chauffeur kids and that's reality of the life as a Mom.

Unfortunately the reality is you can't invent more time but you can be more organized in the time you have.

Have I really sat where you sit now?

Have I really walked in your shoes?

You bet.

I know what you are saying right now.

"I don't have time to get organized. In fact I don't really have time to be reading this book!"

You know the old saying 'It takes money to make money." Same principle applies. It takes time to make more time. It is your choice.

You can take the time to get organized or frankly, you can just go a bit crazy.

The later part is an okay option for a day or two but if your children aren't leaving the nest for another 8 or 10 years, that is a long time to live in chaos.

Being organized or disorganized sets the tone that rules the day for every family. From getting breakfast on the table and the kids out the door to school, to meeting your work goals, to managing your finances and your family time, there is nothing it does not affect.

I dearly love my three children. I wouldn't give up that time with them for anything yet I freely admit that it was some of the most frustrating, annoying to the point of yelling and exhausting to the point of tears, times of my life.

So, it's impossible to always be funny. It is possible to be organized. It is possible to grow-up in an organized home and to teach your children to be organized.

Sure you will still have some frustrating moments but for the most part, you will have a busy but manageable family life.

You know what CHAOS means.

"Can't Have Anybody Over Syndrome."

Are the kitchen counters full of everything that every came out of your car or the mailbox and entered your backdoor? Does the dining room table hold a jigsaw puzzle, random toys, two craft projects and a month's worth of magazines? Do guests find the foyer littered with backpacks and shoes? And what about the kids' rooms? You don't really want me to go there do you?

Have you ever invited in company into the only picked-up room in the house, the living room, and in heated whispers ordered the kids not to give house tours? Or even more common, just stopped having adults come to visit?

Not only are all that clutter and all that stuff managing your life but your children's stuff is managing your life too.

As a professional organizer, I am the person that gets the call to help parents find their desktop, kitchen countertop and the missing floor of the walk-in closet.

These are the truths I know:

You can get rid of clutter.

You can become organized.

Your children can learn personal responsibility for their things.

The family can work together.

It might take a little bit of that time you claim you don't have but in the end, you will find more time to do the things you really want to do.

Chapter 2 Getting Started

Making Your Expectations Meet Reality

Another day equals another load of laundry, you intone.

Sigh.

Ever feel like Michael Keaton in Mr. Mom? Throughout the movie, he is tortured by finding the same dirty T-shirt over and over and over.

"Here," you say, shoving a basket of folded socks, T-shirts, shorts and pajamas into your child's arms. "Take these to your room."

Two days later, you are searching everywhere because all the laundry baskets have vanished. While the house is messy enough to look burglarized, you are pretty sure that no one would take your $4 plastic laundry basket, much less all three that you own. You finally find it in the child's room, still full of the folded laundry.

That, my friend, is a perfect example of expectations meet reality.

You expected the words "take this to your room" to somehow end with the result of the clothes being put away.

Let's say, you actually had a conversation that went more like this "Here, take this to your room AND put them in your dresser."

You remember that dresser don't you? It is the one where the drawers look like they are gagging on the clothes that are half-in and half-out. It is the same one that you took every single thing out of on your day off, two weeks ago, folded it all and sorted it all. Today, you find it back in the same condition as before. Socks in every drawer, T-shirts crammed in the smaller drawer where they don't fit and everything is wrinkled.

That, too, is another example of expectation meets reality.

You expected the words "put them in your dresser" to result in the socks being placed in the sock drawer and the T-shirts in the T-shirt drawer and so on.

That middle ground, following the expectation and preceding the reality, is where the lack of an organizational plan rears its ugly head. Teaching children to be organized means learning how to visualize the steps in any project and break it down to their level.

How many times have you said, or heard someone else say to a child something like "I can't believe you lost it" OR "I can believe you forgot it. You have to learn to be more responsible!" We've all been down that frustration highway.

But consider this:

How many times have you said, or heard someone else say to a child "Let's talk about where your organizing plan went wrong. Let's work on a new strategy for this problem."

This is the difference between our expectations and our reality. The expectation is that the child, no matter the age, has some inborn concept of being organized. The reality is that organization must be taught, practiced and improved upon.

Can children be organized, you wonder? Sometimes when I am speaking, someone will interject "But you haven't seen *my* child!"

Of course I have not seen their child, but I have seen plenty of organized children. Think back to the first time your child had a cubby, at perhaps the church nursery, pre-school or daycare. They dragged you over to see their cubby. They knew exactly which one was theirs and what went in it. At the end of the day, a classroom of 15 three-year olds is not in disarray. Instead, fifteen three-year olds have put their belongings in their cubby and the toys in the right bins.

Simple Tips to Get You Thinking About Working with Children

• Always have them help you organize. Think of it this way... you can often get a child to taste a new food by letting them help you cook the new food.

• For example: Choose a bin together. Gather the items and put them in their new home. Glue a photo or a drawing of the item to the bin. Make it fun.

• It's too much to tackle a whole room with a child. Be patient. Create a home for one thing at a time, with the child participating. Watch them grow in organizing skills. You will soon find them labeling everything!

• Help them learn to organize by adding labels or pictures to your things too.

• Ask them where the items belong. Let them show you. Make it game. You are working to create a habit that will serve them throughout life not find an instant pretty-room fix.

How to Teach Organizing

At preschool, a child knows how to put away toys because they have been told. The toy containers have picture and word labels. They practice it over and over daily and are praised for the tidy room. Their teacher has worked on it and reinforced the organizing.

Let's mentally go back to that basket of laundry.

Most of us went from putting away the child's laundry (and doing everything else) to one day snapping as we are on overload. Something set us off and made us realize they could put it away. We turned and thrust the basket into their hands.

There lies the gap – the missing organizational links. Those links would have included you having them help you clean out that dresser in the first place. If they are big enough to be opening the drawers and messily shoving things in it, they are big enough to sort socks from shirts. The sorting and placing in the drawers process helps reinforce where the items go. Little people forget.

Adding picture labels of socks, undies and so on to the drawers adds a second layer of reinforcing. Going with them several times and supervising or doing the putting away together is the next step.

Finally, praise for doing it properly and helping you is really important. Along with that praise, a healthy dose of reasoning is vital. Tell them that they can get ready on time because they can find everything and because they are organized.

Children can and should, indeed must, learn to be organized.

Chapter 3: Responsibility Issues

Don't Separate Organized & Responsible

You know you're disorganized if …. you find yourself muttering "if you think I'm bad, you should see my mother." This is an example of another one of those it-would-be-funny-if-not-so-sad-moments. It is usually followed by the chants of "I inherited this problem" or "No one ever taught me to be organized." Sure, you thought this book was about getting kids organized. I'm telling you now that a lot of it is about personal responsibility.

Just how, pray tell, do I separate the two? I imagine that if you are reading this, you are just begging for some peace and calm in your home. Would you like a morning without screaming up the stairs or pulling back in the driveway three times for missing items? Do you want your child to make it to the car in the morning, dressed for school complete with a backpack with all the things needed for the day, hair combed, teeth brushed, face shiny, dishes in the dishwasher and a smile on their face?

"Please, is that too much to ask?" you pray, as you once again count to ten and yell things like "Your cleats are in the laundry room where you left them…do you have your library book….and if you are late again, you are not leaving the house this weekend." By the way, adding the words "young lady" is always a good touch to the end of the yell because then they know then we really mean it.

Take a moment and ask yourself this "Are you asking for a more organized child and household or are you asking for a more responsible child?"

In the end, aren't you asking them to be responsible for their own belongings and for their time management? Are you asking them to be organized?

Both! You simply cannot separate the two.

Four Essential Organizing Household Truths

1.

There is a place for everything.

2.

We must always plan ahead to anticipate problems and solutions.

3

Learning to be responsible is learning to be organized.

4

Being a family member means participating in family rules, family chores and family organization. In a family, when a person is being organized, or disorganized, it sets the tone that rules the day for the *whole* family.

Don't Do as I Do, Do as I Say

"You know you are disorganized if …," I joke, in my speeches "Your child starts telling his teacher that his Mom lost his homework." It's so embarrassing. After all, couldn't he cut you a break and say that the dog ate it like every other kid!

Children learn by example, to say the least. Who of us does not have a perfectly horrible example of that fact?

My darling niece demonstrated that one night.

Precious tot that she was, she was in the process of being potty trained and so of course, had some first hand lessons in the bathroom watching Mom. At the same time, she had become totally fascinated with boo-boos and loved to wear and show her bandages on any little scratch.

One evening, she played with her toys as my brother and his wife entertained a lovely dinner party. She had been fed early and changed into pajamas. She wandered into the dining room happily chattering about all of her booboos to everyone, and she was covered in panty liners. She had watched her mom in the bathroom and mirrored pulling off the covering on the tapes. Mimicking Mom, she enjoyed applying them but she stuck them everywhere.

How embarrassing!

Unfortunately, the same is true for disorganization.

How embarrassing!

Kids are going to do what we do. They are going to mimic what you do, good and bad, including that word you'd rather they not use! That also means those piles and piles of paper and clutter you have on countertop, desktop and the lost floor of that walk-in closet, are a far more powerful lessons than your constant fussing about picking up their toys.

Have heart. As you work with your child to become more organized, you will see a ripple effect take place around the house. All is most certainly not lost even if you have clutter up to the top of Mount Vesuvius.

Children also learn by having an organizational lesson. This means taking time to analyze the problem together, coming up with a solution together, and acting on that solution.

As you work through the tips in this book, begin to quietly apply some of the tips to the way you manage your belongings and the spaces for which you are responsible. If you want the little folks to be organized and responsible, remember that they are going to be mirroring you along the way.

Chapter 4: Mistakes of the Disorganized

Just a Mistake Away from Organization

I know that you think you're the only one out there with a little chaos in your daily life and clutter on your brain. You know your disorganized if ..... you have called your own cell phone and then prayed it rang in your purse because then you'd find your purse too.

There are lots of disorganized folks and even those who profess to be organized could always do a bit better in this area or that area. One of the things that separate the two groups is three common disorganized mistakes. Understanding these will help not just you, but it will help you help your family.

1. *The Just For Now Mistake*

When you hear your inner voice says "**just for now**" as you set something down, your hand ought to feel as if it is on fire. It's almost like striking a match but instead you are striking up clutter.

When you hop out of the car and set a load of things in the carport or garage, **just for now**, you start clutter. When you enter the backdoor and empty your pockets and arms, **just for now**, onto the kitchen counter, you start clutter. When you are just too pooped to deal with it anymore and you scoop it all up and shove it in a closet or cabinet**, just for now**, you start clutter.

This is called the **Just for Now** mistake. It is the failure to make a permanent storage decision. Either the items you sat down have a place they belong and you should take them there or they don't have a place and you should make a place for them. Either way, there should not be "just for now" clutter.

2. *Planners without Any Plans*

Shortages of calendars and planners have not been reported on the evening news, so since the supply is plentiful, there must be another reason for a lack of planning.

Everyone has that planner but ***where is the plan***?

Peek inside and there are some doctor appointments, a few ballgames, parent teacher conference, scout meetings, doodles, scribbles and baby drool. No plan in sight.

Often, in completely earnestness we shout "I have got to get organized" and quickly defeat the momentum behind that statement with what I call the Three Horsemen of Disorganization.

- ***Too Much Stuff***
- ***No Home for this Stuff***
- ***No Time to Deal with this Stuff***

Those three horsemen gallop up and effectively make off with your will to get organized. Actually, I think they steal away our ability to make sense.

You can't get organized because you have too much stuff? How are you planning on having less stuff unless you get organized?

You don't have a home for this stuff? Are you planning on not putting it away until you get a bigger home? Do you just intend on walking around it for the next 20 to 30 years or are you just hoping it walks away by itself?

You don't have time to deal with this stuff? That is the best horseman of all. That is the one that fools you into thinking that getting organized steals time, when it really creates time. You waste hours and days and weeks losing things, finding things, hunting for things, cleaning around over and under things and all that time, moving that stuff from point A to point B and back again. You don't have time ***not*** to deal with this situation.

It's time to pull out that planner and make an actual written plan, step-by-step, to get organized. Along the way in this book, you'll find concrete advice on how to do just that. For now, what you need to know is that you need a plan in your planner!

3. *Organizing Clutter Mistake*

Try as you might, you simply cannot organize clutter. It can't be done.

Don't tell my youngest daughter. She's tried to organize clutter for years. Pretty soon every bit of storage space in her room was full. She had a moderate sized walk-in closet that included a double hanging bar and some shelving. The shelves were full of stacks of neatly line-up shoe boxes. She has a tall, antique iron bed and underneath it, were more neatly stacked boxes.

Eventually, there were stacks of things in the corners of the room and a jumble of shoes and accessories in the closet floor. She'd fuss that there was no where to place any of it. Meanwhile, she was adrift in a sea of photos and photo albums, scrapbooking materials, hats, shoes, magazines, CDs and assorted flotsam and jetsam of teenage life.

I'd pause at the doorway of her room – the hardest room for me to avoid because our rooms are across the hall from each other - and she'd be sitting in a sea of stuff.

"I thought you came in here to clean up your room," I'd ask.

"I did clean up my room," she'd insist. "I have no room for these things."

Soon I'd be in the room trying to rearrange the boxes in the closet. Some felt pretty light or heavy for shoes, so I opened them for a peek. You couldn't help but laugh.

"What is this stuff," I'd ask holding out the open box.

The box would be filled with all manner of objects. A typical inventory would include a half-eaten pack of gum, breath mints, folded notes passed in class, empty CD case, two hard disks of unknown content, a Happy Meal toy still in plastic, several board game pieces, a partial deck of cards, bobby pins, sample bottle of lotion, cardboard holder from an earring purchase, some junk mail, photo of the dog, a couple of coins, beads from a broken bracelet and a colored turkey from Thanksgiving, vintage age five.

See, she did not have any storage space because she attempted to organize clutter. All of the valuable space was taken by junk.

Trying to organize clutter is one of the biggest organizing mistakes. I've seen adult friends and neighbors try it too.

Where I live, we have rows and rows of plastic tubs and storage items at the office supply store, the department store and the home improvement store. In fact, what store doesn't have a wealth of plastic tubs for sale? Trying to organize clutter accounts for millions and millions in sales. Everyone wants to purchase things for getting organized.

Not too long ago I was heading into a big discount store and out came an acquaintance, her cart piled high with plastic tubs and lids.

"Hey, what are you up to," I asked.

"I'm going to get organized," she grinned.

"What are you putting in all of those?"

"Oh my gosh. I have got so much stuff. You just can't imagine how much stuff I have," she said. Leaning in closer, she confided "I just can't get rid of anything."

It's sad but true that when she gets home, she will not be any more organized than she was prior to her purchase. She will still have too much stuff- but it will all nicely be encased in plastic. All she did was organize her clutter. It was just another version of my daughter's shoe box collection.

As a professional organizer, I've gone to a client's home, and after a tour, I have declared that the problem is TMS- Too Much Stuff.

Too Much Stuff - TMS Disease!

Not once have I ever gone to a client's home and declared that they had just the right amount of stuff but what they really needed were more organizing products and more plastic tubs!

You can't organize clutter. It simply can't be done.

* As a footnote, let me add a humorous and hopeful note. The young daughter who struggled trying to organize closet clutter is now a talented and fabulous young lady in the fashion industry – and I love that her first work desk was actually in a huge fashion closet that she was paid to keep organized!

Chapter 5: GO- Get Organized

Getting in the Right Mindset to GO! (Get Organized)

By now, I doubt you need any more motivation to get organized at home. Still I want you to know the average person wastes an hour a day looking for things that they know they have but don't know where they have them!

Not me, you say!

How about the three trips into the house for one more thing before you could really get out the drive this morning? How about the two phone calls to get the address you wrote down on the edge of something and now you can't find it? How about the cries of "Mom! Where are my shoes?" Or hairbrush? Or homework?

How long do you spend look for things each day?

There are some tricks of the trade to having an organized household. I've talked about clutter because you simply can't start having new rules of responsibility and new techniques for getting and staying organized if every room is in a sea of clutter. Your child simply can't grasp how to keep their dresser or their room tidy if there are things everywhere. You will need to begin with a clean sweep.

Working to get rid of the clutter everywhere, you will create an environment easier to maintain.

To get started, the things you have to pitch out are those clutter obstacles, the stumbling blocks that keep you in disarray.

First get rid of your clutter obstacles

- I might need it someday
- I can't throw anything away
- I'm creative
- I'm a perfectionist
- I won't be able to keep it up
- I've always done it that way

Do those clutter obstacles sound familiar?

They should. Those obstacles are a popular refrain of the disorganized.

One of the biggest of organizing mistakes is trying to organize clutter and that one is backed up by making a lot of excuses for that clutter.

Think about how these excuses hold up to closer examination.

- ***I might need it someday*** – all of the "someday" items are today's clutter. If you don't know exactly when you will need it, then out it goes.
- ***I can't throw anything away*** – ask yourself what is the worst thing that would happen to you if you got rid of that item. Most likely you can let it go.
- ***I'm creative*** – If you are saying that your creative brain doesn't do organizing, remember that is just an excuse. Creativity and organizing go hand in hand. You will have plenty of ways to be creative in thinking of fun ideas that will keep your family organized or fun ways to keep belongings. Thinking outside the box will really make this work for you.

- ***I'm a perfectionist*** - No one wants you to be perfect- certainly not me and not your family. Being organized is about living more peacefully and enjoying your home and family. It is not at all about looking like a magazine shoot.
- ***I won't be able to keep it up*** – Yes, you will be able to keep it up. As mentioned above, it is not about being perfect. It is about making systems and ways that work for your family. It is not about designing something that doesn't work the way you think. If you tackled an organizing project in the past that didn't work for you, it doesn't mean that all projects won't work for you. It means THAT one wasn't right for your family. I always say "Good enough is grand." This means that it doesn't have to be grand. It just has to be good enough.
- ***I've always done it that way***- Sometimes I hear this after new ideas are offered. Think of the TV guru Doctor Phil. He always smiles and says to his guests "So, how has that been working for you?"

Chapter 6: Quieting the Clatter of Clutter

Love it, Use it, Need it

Want to get organized? Want to find your belongings? Then get rid of your clutter excuses and then get rid of the clutter.

Make your clutter sorting easy. Ask yourself :

Love it?

Use it?

Need it?

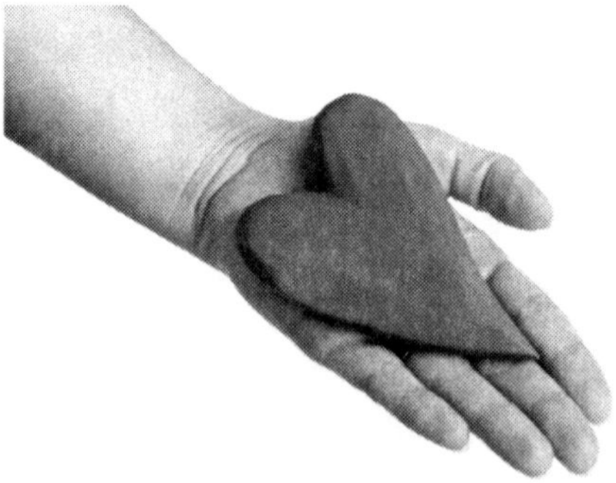

Everything must fit one of those. Why would you keep anything in your house that you don't love, use or need?

Creating the Clutter Removal Plan

Later in this book, I'll give you specific ideas for children's needs and children's rooms. However, if you have overall clutter issues, you need to begin to work on those first. Here are some basic tips for any cluttered area.

Hatch out a new organizational plan for your troubled areas.

Don't know where to start? I promise you it is more important to start than to spend any time worrying about where to start. Got more than one troubled spot? Just pick one and follow these basic guidelines.

1) Decide which room or area to work on and stick to it until completion. No bouncing between areas.
2) Plan ahead a reward for completing the job.
3) Give yourself a deadline in writing on your calendar. Be realistic.
4) Break your troubled area into small zones or amounts of time.

For example, a guest bedroom may have a desk, under the bed, on the bed, a bookshelf and a closet- with a upper shelf, a bar, a closet floor, to organize. Each of those areas are zones. Grab your calendar or planner and write down enough appointments with yourself to finish one zone. If 30 minutes is all you can give to the job that is fine, just make yourself enough 30 minutes appointments to complete the job.

5) Keep the appointments with yourself!

6) Get trash bags and empty boxes. Label boxes: Give to Charity; Take to new location or; Trash; Shred etc.

*Mom-to-Mom Tip!

At the end of this book, you will find printable labels for your sorting boxes!

7) Set a timer or alarm clock for 30 minutes. Put on some music so you can sing along. Begin on your project area. Work left to right. Sort clutter into trash bags or the appropriate box. Choose one location to stack everything that will stay in the room or leave it where it sits but remove surrounding clutter.

8) At the end of each day's appointment, shred documents, take the trash bags out, place donations on the FRONT SEAT of your car and distribute your box of items that belong in other rooms. Stop. The rest of your day is your own.

9) Repeat steps on your next appointments.

10) When done decluttering: Return to room. Organize remaining items. Put like items together. Give decluttered room a good cleaning.

Give yourself that reward. You deserve it.

Chapter 6: Children's Bedrooms

You call this a bedroom? Where's the bed!

As a professional organizer, people practically taunt me when asking me to "do something with my child's room."

"Are they really disorganized," I ask.

Yes! There is stuff everywhere. You need a rake to get

under the bed. The piles keep you from opening the door or from closing the door."

That my parent friends, has nothing to do with being organized.

Sorry but it's true.

Being disorganized is the inability to meet deadlines. The child can not find their school work, workbooks or homework. There are never two shoes that match available when it is time to run out of the house. You have to buy multiples of soccer shin guards and athletic supporters. Your child is never ready on time and if they are ready, there is a litany of things they do not have with them and there is always an excuse. It is never their fault. "He made me late. She didn't tell me. Mom didn't give it to me." Sound familiar?

That is disorganized.

Despite the unmade bed, clothes and toys on the floor and drifts of school papers, if they are responsible enough to meet deadlines and manage their time well, then they are organized. Maybe messy, but still they are organized.

It is very important to understand the difference. Both types of children can learn tricks to living in a more orderly environment with a place for everything and things in their place. However, the disorganized child must learn so much more. It is not just their space that needs some work, but the way they think and the way the function must be analyzed.

Have your tried different bedroom mess-management techniques? These range from the close-the-door and pretend the room isn't there plan to the you-will-clean-it every-day-or-no-TV plan to the let them wallow like pigs in their own mess and they will get sick of it plan. How about the let it build up until YOU explode plan?

Been there. Tried all of those personally.

When my son was about nine, I was tired of the enforcer game and decided he could just suffer the consequences. If his room was messy, then that was his problem. It became a ritual to walk down the hall and shut the door without looking. Call it a battle of wills. "I bet I can hold out longer than he does," was my thought.

Boy was I wrong.

One day, I headed down the hall and the smell almost killed me.

This is not a gross exaggeration, it is just gross. There certainly exists what moms' know to be that sweaty little boy scent which grows to be the teenage sneaker, sweat socks and wet towel smell. Nope. This was something different.

I kicked some things out of the way and stumbled my way across the room and zeroed in on the hamster cage.

Thomas Edison, a short-haired hamster, enjoyed a vigorous life of racing through Habitrails® and building block mazes and feasting on all matter of things from bell pepper cores to nacho chips. He was nestled in the wood shavings on the floor of the cage, which sat on the desk directly next to my son's bed. If his cage had been milk, it was at least two weeks past expiration date!

About two feet from my son's pillow, poor Thomas wallowed in wet cedar chips.

It is in my memory that screaming was involved. Only a nine-year-old boy can fully love a hamster and not notice a smelly cage!

"Smell what?" was the reply from the son.

"How could you live in here with that smell, son?"

"I didn't notice."

Now how in the world could this bright child not notice? I learned that if you are not going to notice a smelly hamster next to your pillow, you are not going to take note of the state of the rest of your room. Waiting for the ah-ha moment in room cleaning was not going to happen. Clearly the wait-until-the-child-can't-stand-it technique didn't work. Neither did the wait-until-Mom-explodes technique didn't work either!

What to do?

Bedroom Attack Master Plan!

Where do parents start when they have a kids' closet or room that looks like a tornado has swept through and created a national disaster?

Start with a good attitude. If the room overwhelms you, imagine being half your size! If you get frustrated and take over, you have taught the child some important lessons. You have taught them they were right and it is too hard for them, which is not true, and that if they mess up, they can get out of the chore altogether.

Plan to work together.

Plan to take a break. Tell the child you are going to work together and choose a time for a snack and break. Keep things pleasant.

Put on some fun music. Gather boxes or bags and label them "Trash,

Uh Oh!

Oh no you didn't!

Did you really use your child's closet to store your winter clothing or gift wrap? Do you have the shelves stuffed with things you didn't know what to do with?

If you are teaching them about respect for the space of others, such as not leaving their toys all over the place, then you can't use their space. If you want them to have storage space for their things and learn personal responsibility then it is time for you to fess up. Remove your items from their closet. If you have too much stuff for your own closet, it is time to get real with yourself!

Donate, Put in a New Spot." (You'll find some printable labels at the back of this book.) Grab a laundry basket, a broom and a few cleaning supplies. Now you are ready for the step-by-step. Remember, the child is doing all of these tasks ***with you***. You might even copy this checklist, give it to them let them be the boss and you be the worker-bee.

Clearing Out Clutter

Means Asking Some Hard Questions!

Why would I need it?

When would I need it again?

Who would ask me for it? (Give it to them now.)

When did I use it last?

And, for those who "can't throw anything away…"
"What is the worst thing that could happen to me if I got rid of this?

- Gather all the clothes lying about. Head to the laundry room with them. Turn on washer.
- Make the bed- you might need the surface for sorting.
- Any dishes? Head to the kitchen.
- Use the broom to pull out items under the bed and furniture.
- Collect toys from furniture tops and place with pile on floor.

- From the floor and surfaces, gather all the books, papers and schoolwork and place in one stack.
- Grab big toys and put away. Evaluate toys as you go. If broken or outgrown, place in the correct box. If something doesn't belong in this room, put it in the "put in a new spot" box.
- Take the broom and sweep everything to one side. On the clean side, begin to sort the items such as dolls, cars and trucks, puzzle pieces. Continue evaluating if the toy needs to be kept. Once sorted, stow away properly.
- Don't forget your snack break! Don't forget to enjoy this time talking with your child.
- Sort and file away school papers and books.
- Take the trash out. Place the donation items in the car. Take the move-me stack to the right locations.
- Dust and vacuum together. You are never too young to learn these skills!
- Take the time to create labels that will help the child keep up their room organized.

Stop! Focus and Finish!

Be aware of projects within projects!

Suppose you are organizing your desk. You dig in and find photos. Next thing you know, you have dug out photo albums and are putting in photos. You have totally left your project of desk organizing for photo organizing.

Key words: **Focus and Finish**! Focus on the project at hand. Finish the project at hand. When you find a project with an organizing project, set it aside. Add it to your to-do list and go back to focus and finish the original project.

This applies to children's rooms and teaching children to be organized too. Help them learn to **focus and finish.** When you come across things in their room that take you off track, remember to focus and finish and come back to those items later.

The alternative is to have everything started and nothing completed.

Tips to remember in the Bedroom Attack Master Plan

- Work in small increments of time.
- Teach the child but don't do it all for them.
- Purge out old toys, outgrown clothes and junk.
- Decide TOGETHER how to organize the rest.
- Purchase storage items as needed.
- Label. Label. Label.
- Help. Encourage. Reward. Don't Take Over.
- With your child's help and suggestions, make cleaning and organizing rules to prevent future chaos. (See next section for ideas)

Chapter 7: Staying Tidy

Keeping Up with the Cleaning Up

"But I DID clean my room!"

This is the opportunity for parents to roll their own eyes back in their head until they get stuck! Clearly, our version of clean and their version of clean are like reading a book compared to watching the movie about the book. The characters don't look at all like we imagined and the ending isn't even close!

This is because yet again our expectations have met reality. We once again assumed that our children would understand what the words "Clean your room" mean.

They don't.

Once again, you can become their personal organizer until they leave for college. You can send them back to make the bed. Then you can send them back to clean under the bed. Then you can send them back to get the trash. Are you worn out yet? Every time you bring up yet another thing to be done, there are bound to be protests or bargaining or reasons why they can't do it. So you are beating your head against the wall every step of the way.

Following the usage of the ***Bedroom Attack Master Plan*** is the time to develop a plan to maintain the organized room. Before you sit-down with your child to develop a cleaning/organizing plan for the future, you need to have a little conversation with yourself.

Everyone has a different idea of what clean means. Everyone has a different idea of what level of clutter or chaos they can live with. If you want your child to live up to certain standards in your house, you need to think about what those standards are for you. You also need to take into consideration the needs of the child for use of the room.

Most parents seem to understand that it is not healthy to let a TV or video game become their child's companion. The best counter to those activities is time and space for imaginative play.

Take the time to interact with your child in the middle of what you might consider to be a gigantic mess. Sit down on the floor and engage them in some conversation and you'll find that the blocks in various corners of the room are forts on different islands. The Barbie clothing in piles under the desk is the "mall." There can be a lot going on that is imaginative play rather than a mess. On the other hand, six board games dumped on the floor is indeed a mess!

For my children, I decided that a clean room needed to occur only once per week. Between school, homework and sports, there wasn't a ton of free play time. By the time they got the imaginary city set up or the Barbie dolls dressed, it could be bedtime. They had more play time if I let the play extend over a number of days. Instead of nagging daily about the room, consider having some daily rules that control the mess and consider cleaning up toys on a regular basis, perhaps once per week, rather than daily.

Setting Some Ground Rules

Here are some ideas for bedroom and playroom rules that you can tweak to match your household and your standards.

> **Do A Little At a Time**
>
> If you try the once-a-week room cleaning technique and ***find your child is overwhelmed***, break it into mini-tasks. For example, they could gather and put away books and videos. Later they could hunt up all the dirty or clean clothing and put it away. Then they might tackle all the things with wheels and so forth.
>
> Sometimes, as adults, we put off organizing because we think we need a huge chunk of time to get the project completed. When this happens to your child, help guide them into ***dividing the room and doing a little at a time.***

What do you want done daily? Just because toys are left out, for imaginary play, it doesn't mean everything must be in a state of chaos. Some daily expectations might include:

- Bath towels returned to bathroom and hung up.
- Dirty clothing in hamper.

- Clean clothing or jackets hung up. Shoes put away- always key so a pair can be found in a hurry.
- Dishes/snacks returned to kitchen or not eaten in the room.

Talk about the use of personal space. Part of the clutter in a household comes from each family member thinking they can leave their belongings all over the place. In some ways, you can allow their room to the THEIR space. The rules you set there, such as cleaning once each week, are rules for their personal space. That doesn't mean they can leave their belongings all over the house and only pick them up once per week. Different rules can apply to different rooms as well as to different family members. An older child will need help understanding that their toddler sister leaves toys around but that doesn't make it okay for them to leave toys in the living room since they are old enough to understand.

Make a check list of what you expect when you ask them to clean up their room. (Suggestions for age appropriate chores follow this section.) Clearly a young child will only have some of these items on their list and a middle or high school child should be doing the entire list.

Some ideas that might be on your list include:

- Toys picked up and put away.
- Nothing under the bed.
- Clean clothes put away.
- Top of furniture dusted.
- Clean sheets on the bed.
- Bed made.
- Mirror shined.
- Desk cleaned off of accumulated papers and books.
- Sports equipment stowed away properly.
- Vacuum ran.
- Trash emptied.

Use a wipe-off board to list chores appropriate for their age. The child can check off the items as they do them instead of you being the enforcer. Once they are checked, they can then show you what they have done.

Take the time to do chores with your child, praising them along the way. Examples for little helpers: You can control the spray can of furniture polish and they can use the rag to make the furniture shiny. You can hold the big trash bag and they can help dump the trash into it. You can change the sheets and they can drag the dirty ones to the laundry room.

Doing the chores for them, instead of with them, takes away time to spend laughing and having a conversation with the child. It takes away that chance to teach them to be responsible for their personal space. At that moment, it may be faster and more efficient for you to do it. The key words there are *at that moment.* All of those moments that you did it could have been spent teaching them how to do it themselves.

***Mom-to-Mom Tip**

Store the spare sheets in your child's room. Then they don't have to search a linen closet for the right-size set.

Remember that cleaning a child's room has many lessons in organization. It teaches them how to use the space. How to put like items together. How to plan your day and your time to make room for the things that need to be done. It teaches them skills they will use their entire life.

If you are lucky enough to be able to afford a cleaning service, don't let your child off the hook in the responsibility area. At the very least, they should put their dirty and clean clothing away and pick up all the toys so that the cleaning person can dust and vacuum. A good household rule is that if they cannot do the basics, allowing the housekeeper to get in their room and clean, then the child must do the cleaning themselves.

Finally, remember the old adage about picking your battles carefully. There are many more important battles than a tidy room. (Can you believe a professional organizer would say that?!) I'd much rather focus on the importance of education – getting homework done and getting studying accomplished. I'd much rather focus on respect for adults – teachers, parents, grandparents. I'd much rather focus on manners. Find a happy medium that you and the child can live with. If you are going to choose a daily battle, make sure it is an important one.

Here are some ideas, by age, of when a child might be able to help with chores in their room.

Toddler:

Drops clothing into hamper and toys into bins- with your help and encouragement. Clap and sing and make it fun.

Ages 3 to 5

Toys into bins.

Clothing into Hamper.

Help you in matching clean laundry with correct drawer.

Wipe furniture after you have sprayed the furniture polish.

Crawl under bed or other furniture to retrieve lost toys.

Ages 6 to 10

Above list plus mirror shined, with your help.

Sports equipment put away properly.

Trash can empty.

Dishes/snacks to kitchen if allowed to eat in room.

School papers and books put away. (Note: See special chapter on teaching children to put away paperwork.)

Makes bed.

*Mom-to-Mom Tip!

Choose a puffy comforter instead of a bedspread. It is much more forgiving if the sheets and blankets are lumpy and wrinkled underneath. It lets the child make the bed without you fussing about remaking it neatly.

Age 11 and Up

Everything above plus:

Change sheets and put on clean ones.

Run vacuum. Note: You should supervise and make sure that there are no small items to suck up and damage the vacuum and take the time to teach your child how to operate the vacuum properly and safely. At first, you may need to finish up the vacuuming around the edges or point out where they missed. Older children and teens should be able to run a vacuum. Remember, they manage all those buttons on computers and video games just fine!

You can't expect a child to be organized if there is nowhere to put anything.

Sometimes as parents, we forget to recognize that a child's physical space is much more difficult than our own room. We may have clothes and books but they have clothes, books, homework, sports equipment, hobbies, computers, televisions, games, and toys of all descriptions crammed into their space.

In order for a child to keep order, they need some good basic equipment. Without places for easy storage, the words "clean your room" are simply overwhelming.

While you don't need to run out and spend a fortune on organizing products, you can't organize a child's room without some of the organizing essentials. In an early chapter, I mentioned that most people suffer from TMS, Too Much Stuff, rather than suffer from a lack of organizing products. While that remains true, there are indeed some staples of a child's room that will help with room organization.

Great Solutions: A Child's Room Checklist

□ Shelves for books

□ Bins of different sizes for different sized toys

□ Shelves for board games

□ Low rod in closet for young children

□ Shoe holders for shoes

□ Labels on drawers (picture of item for young non-readers)

□ Lots of coat hooks for jackets, robes, sports equipment/uniforms, book bags

□ Bulletin boards- bigger the better, 2 or 3 in a tight row is great unless you love having them tape and tack to the wall!

□ File crate or small file cabinet (a later chapter will help you with paperwork organizing)

□ Hamper or hanging mesh laundry bag

*Mom-to-Mom Tip! Collectables & Keepsakes!

Does your child have collectable dolls or sports trophies? Items that are beloved but not necessarily played with can really take up the small amount of space available on a desk or dresser. Add a shelf across one wall of the room. Place the shelf just above the door frame, so it is about 24 inches from the ceiling. This allows plenty of display space for special items, also protecting them if they are fragile, and keeps surfaces clutter free.

Top 10 Tips for Organizing Your Child's Room

1. Keep safety in mind. Children will climb up on things. Make sure that furniture, such as bookcases and heavy dressers are properly secured to the wall. (You'll find many directions on the Internet for childproofing a room. That is the number one priority before organizing.)
2. Be sure that no items of danger are within reach.
3. Place like items together.
4. Place commonly used items within reach.
5. Place seldom used items on higher or lower shelves.
6. Place items in which you want parental control, such as finger-paint or puzzles with many pieces, on high shelves or even out of the room in another location.
7. Label everything.
8. Establish household rules, such as only one board game or puzzle may be taken out at a time.
9. Leave floor space for a place to play.
10. Consider putting some toys away and swapping every so often with the ones that are currently in use.

Great Tips for Kids, Rooms and Toys

Toddler Toy Overload

Due to the generosity of parents, grandparents, birthday parties and holidays; young children's rooms often are a sea of toys. Children can become overwhelmed with the clutter and with the lack of play area. Get several boxes and fill them with a portion of the toys. Move the boxes to the top of the closet or other storage area. After a couple of months, renew interest by taking out the stored toys, which are fresh and new again to the child, and then box up some of the other toys. This method keeps the child's interest, reduces clutter and makes more room to really play.

*Mom-to-Mom Tip!

Add a note to your calendar that reminds you to switch the toys!

Toys, Books, Animals, Clutter and More

Everyone is suffering from what I call TMS disease, or Too Much Stuff. It is the biggest challenge facing parents. The parents and children continue to acquire more stuff with the in-flow always greater than the out-flow. With stuff always coming into the home but never out of the home, it is not surprising we simply are surrounded with clutter. The biggest challenge facing parents is to learn to be more moderate with the amount of toys and belongings. How to begin? Practice the one-in, one-out rule. For every new toy or book coming in, have the child choose a toy or book he or she has outgrown. Teach them to be generous to the less fortunate by donating to charity or teach them about money by having a garage sale.

*Mom-to-Mom Tip!

Start a donation box or bag so that you always have a spot to collect items.

Legos® and More Legos®

There is a great sorter and storage system for this fun toy. Drop all the pieces in the top and it sorts them by shape. This is great for the younger children. You can see the Lego® sorter at http://www.box4blox.com/ .

As you advance to older children, who own many sophisticated pieces, you might like this great Lego idea that comes from my sister. Cut out a large circle from a piece of sturdy fabric. Hem the edge. Add button holes or grommet holes, spaced around the edge. Thread a piece of cord through the holes, creating a draw string bag that can be laid out flat. Lay it out for a Lego® playing mat. When playtime it over, pull the string and gather up all the pieces. Hang the drawstring bag from a hook until the next play time. This technique will work with any toy that has many pieces.

Other Unique Organizing Ideas

The over-the-door shoe holder, with clear pockets, is my very favorite organizing gadget. I will confess that I have never put shoes into one. The back of the bedroom or closet door is unused space. Turn it into an art center by filling the pockets with art goodies lying about. For a girl's room, it is great to corral accessories from scarves and purses to belts and all those ponytail holders. It can hold video games, CD's, socks, 24 or more Barbie dolls and her wardrobe or anything you can imagine.

It's a Matter of Control

We all want to be in control. Kids too! That is why we end up in a power struggle. One of the best organizing tips for working with children is to allow them input. Ask them all kinds of questions and really listen.

How did your room get this way?

What kind of room rules would help keep it more organized?

Where should you keep your books?

Allowing your child some say in their room layout really makes them feel in charge of their room. Once they feel in charge, they will feel empowered to take care of their room. Let them suggest a new arrangement for the furniture. It might not be as an interior decorator would do it but who cares! A decorator doesn't live in the room. Let them rearrange the furniture, as long as the choice is safe and doesn't block exits. Let them choose a wall color or a new comforter for the bed. Take into consideration their suggestions for how and where to store their toys. Remember that if that decision doesn't work out, you can point out that it didn't work out and ask them to come up with a new idea. Part of getting and staying organized is accepting change. As things change, you must change with them. If something doesn't work out, then try something new!

Empowering your kids with choices in their own room, at the same time as giving them responsibility for that rooms' cleaning and organization, is a win-win situation. Again, you can't sit back and order them to do it. Every step of teaching your child to be organized is a cooperative effort between parent and child.

Chapter 8: Children's Closets

Controlling Closet Chaos

Outgrown Clothing:

Children's closets differ from adult closets. Their closets reflect that they continue to grow. (Ok, sometimes our closets reflect that we continue to grow but let's not get into that!) The typical infant-toddler-child closet will contain clothes that are too big, waiting for them to grow into them, and clothes they have outgrown.

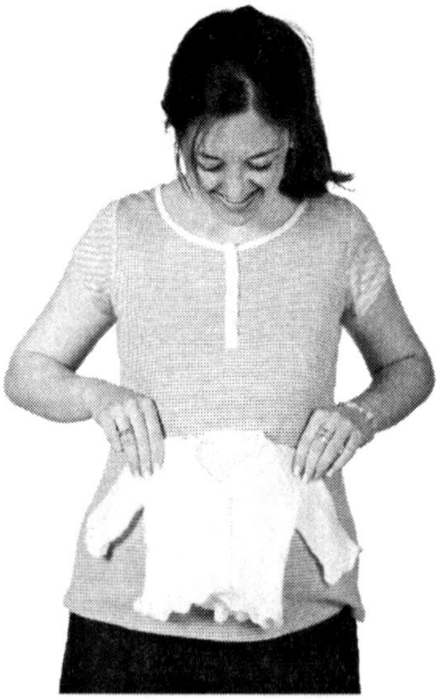

Here are some tips to plan for these stages: Add a tall plastic hamper or lidded-kitchen trash can to the corner of the closet. As your baby or child outgrows clothing, you now have a place for those outgrown items. Drop the clean items into the hamper.

When the hamper is full, you have several choices. If you want to save the clothing for a future sibling or other relative, then remove the hamper from the closet. Label it with the sizes (example: *Newborn to 6 Months*) and place the hamper in the attic. Don't write on the hamper as you will use it again in the future for perhaps another size. Tape or tie on a tag. The hamper is already packed with clean clothing and sorted by size so it makes your work easy. Place a new hamper in the closet. It is no more expensive to do this than to buy a plastic tub for storage- which would take up a lot more room and not be nearly as easy to use.

If you don't have a need for the clothing, load it into your car and take it to a donation center or a consignment shop and empty it. Return the empty hamper to the closet.

Larger Sized Clothing:

Often, we come across a darling baby outfit buried in the closet and are disappointed because the child has already outgrown it.

"But it still has the tags on it," we cry.

Avoid this by making some hanging bar tags. Attach labels to extra hangers. Use the labels to divide your hanging bar into 3 month, 6 month, 9 month, and 12 month sizes. This will help you make the most use out of gifts or purchases you found on sale.

For folding clothes that are too large, take the time to sort them by size. You can use any container- plastic bags, shopping bags, tubs, baskets, laundry baskets or extra dresser drawer- just make sure that you place a label with the size on the container. I've seen many moms have to sit down and sort bags over and over because they couldn't remember what sizes it held.

Remember, good choices for organizing means making everyday items easy to reach. Place items you use often in areas that you don't have to sit on the floor to find or have to climb up and find - that means basically between your shoulders and your knees. Those too-big clothes are not accessed often. These items are perfect to go on the top shelf of the closet.

Look at Things from a Child's Eyes

When you child-proof a home, experts tell us to crawl around and look at dangers that a child might see from their low height. If you want your child to be organized, you also need to look at organizing needs from their height. Too often, household items, such as towel bars in the bathroom, are not useable for a child.

For a child, who is young but old enough to dress themselves, the closet hanging bar is most likely out of reach. In organizing sections of stores and on-line, you can purchase a bar that hangs from the primary rod. It creates a second, lower level. This not only doubles your hanging space but it creates a low area the child can reach.

> **In most homes, a child's closet holds things besides clothing. They may have board games, dress-up clothing or other toys in the closet.**

When organizing the double bar, place the outfits that you are happy with your child wearing on their lower bar. On the upper bar, place the large outfits they have yet to grow into as well as dressy or special occasion clothing you don't want worn on a daily basis.

Add some coat hooks, either in the closet or perhaps on the back of the bedroom door. This makes it easy for them to have a place they can reach for jackets, hats, umbrellas and the like. If you add a basket to one of the hooks, they will have a place for gloves and mittens.

Children typically don't own a lot of shoes as they outgrown them so quickly. It is important for them to learn early that shoes do have a home. A small basket in the closet for shoes is appropriate for youngsters. As they get older, do add some shoe shelves.

One of the things that I recognize as an organizer is that the floor is a magnet.

If one item is on the floor, another lands there. Then another and another. Pretty soon, there is a closet floor full of clutter. If the shoes are on the floor, then why not a hat? Or umbrella? Or some books? Maybe some school papers? Puzzle pieces? It goes on and on as the child (and adults too) figure if one thing, even shoes, can be on the floor so can dozens of things. Having a home for everything, even shoes, is the best prevention for floor pile-ups.

In most homes, a child's closet holds things besides clothing. They may have board games, dress-up clothing or other toys in the closet. Be sure to place all of the real clothing and accessories on one side of the closet. Use the other side for storage of the toys and other items. Eventually, as the child is older and needs more clothing storage, you won't have room for toys. If you want to add some shelves to the closet for toy and game storage, do so with some that are not installed to the wall. I've found you can find easy-assemble shelving to fit in most closets and it can be removed and another use found in future years as the child outgrows toys and games.

Remember, you are teaching your child to be organized and that everything has a place. These lower, well-thought out storage areas are not just so they can help themselves get dressed but so that they can be responsible in putting items away by themselves.

Remember to add labels, using pictures for nonreaders.

Chapter 9: Chores

The Challenge of Organizing Chores

> **Remember the Essential Organizing Household Truths**
>
> Being a family member means participating in family rules, ***family chores*** and family organization. In a family, when a person is being organized, or disorganized, it sets the tone that rules the day for the *whole* family.

"Whatever you do, don't share the chore bowl story," cautioned my youngest daughter.

"Did you really hate it so much," I asked.

"No, I'm just trying to protect kids from chores," she said laughing. But then she added that she was planning to do the same thing when she has kids someday. This young lady can clean a house, cook a meal, do laundry, balance a checkbook, iron, mend, garden and mow a lawn.

Everybody has a different opinion on chores and just like all parenting, there is no right or wrong - there is just different.

From my perspective as a professional organizer and mother, I can tell you that I think that chores are really, really important.

Don't Take the Lazy Way Out

The lazy way of assigning chores is to give each child permanent chores. Suppose you tell your son that it is his permanent job to collect the trash and pull the can to the curb. What has he learned from that? He is now a great trash collector but he doesn't know how to load the dishwasher, rake the leaves, cook a piece of chicken or wash his uniform. You are sending him out into the world knowing how to take out the trash!

Share the chores. Every child should learn the things necessary to running a household and taking personal responsibility for themselves. The more variety to the chores, the more self-sufficient and confident they will be when they leave home.

Here are some of the top excuses for adults who are cluttered and disorganized-

I bet you have heard these or maybe said them yourself.

No one taught me to be organized.

If you think I'm bad, you should see my mother.

I don't know how to do it.

I don't know where to start.

Today's schooling typically does not include home economics for boys or girls. If you are going to learn to clean a bathroom, vacuum, mop a floor, do laundry, sew on a button, make a menu and grocery list, run a lawn mower, iron a shirt and so on- you have to learn at home. If you are going to learn time management- how to have and keep a job, have groceries in the house, keep the house clean and the lawn cut plus find time for friends and family- where are you going to learn it? You are going to learn it in your childhood home.

You are doing your child no favors by thinking you are doing a favor by doing all the housework for them. Every child should have a few chores to do- weekly or daily- or both. You are teaching time management, household organization, good sanitation for a healthy life, life skills and personal responsibility. On top of all those lessons, you will find that you are a better parent.

If you are run ragged doing every chore yourself, how do you find time to play with your child, help with homework or have a date or a quiet moment with your spouse?

Think your child can't tackle household chores? Think again! Even a three year old can stand on a step stool and put away clean silverware or pour food in the kitty's bowl.

I had my children do a chore or two each day – sometime between after school and dinner- whatever fit their day. As a fulltime-working mom, I can tell you that having them each do two small things- meant six things I did not have to do. This helped me to not let household organization get out of control.

If my three children each had two after-school chores, it made all our lives easier. Here's an example of six things that would take them five minutes each to do them but would take me 30 minutes to do them for them.

- Water the plants on the porch.
- Walk the dog.
- Feed the pets.

- Empty the dishwasher.
- Wipe the glass tabletops in the den
- Set the table.

Sometimes on a busy weekend, I would wonder ***how I was going to get through one football game, two soccer games, cheerleading practice, church, youth group and a slumber party, pay bills, buy groceries, do laundry and clean house.????????***

I would tell the family that they all had to help. Out would come the chore bowl. I'd make a master list of everything that needed to be accomplished. That included all kinds of things from wipe kitchen counters to mop floor to shake rugs to dust the den. I'd cut the list into strips and fold them. I'd drop them into bowls and everyone would draw out the same number.

I put the harder chores- such as mop the floor in one bowl and easier chores- such as shake out the rugs in another bowl. Then depending on how many there was to do, I'd have each child- ***and parent***- draw the same number. For example, we might draw two hard and three easy apiece. Then, we would all work to get it all done. The random drawing eliminated all the arguing about" why did you made me do this" and "I had to do this last time." Plus, working with the parents sets a great example of team work and family responsibility.

*Mom-to-Mom Tip!

On a daily basis, it is a good idea for staying organized to assign each family member a room besides their own. They gather everything out of place in that room and return it to the right spot.

*Mom-to-Mom Tip!

Sometimes, there might be a parent-only chore that the kids can't handle. If so, include that in your chores but simply announce that instead of drawing your first chore, you are choosing to do the adult-only chore while they draw from the chore bowl.

My child can do THAT?

Your child can do chores of all kinds. ***Remember, chores should be done as a family.*** Everyone shares in the work and shares in the fun in a family. Many chores involve cleaning supplies, tools or appliances that use electricity. For safety sake, be sure you take the time to demonstrate the proper use of each item and supervise the child doing chores. Note: You'll find tips for laundry in a special chapter of this book.

*Mom-to-Mom Tip!

Find a way for your very young child to be your "helper." They can put socks away while you do the rest of the laundry basket. They can get the sippee cups out of the dishwasher. They can have a dusting rag or sponge and "help" you.

Following, you will find a list of the kinds of chores a child might do by age. Clearly not every chore needs doing every day- or even every week. This list is to give you ideas. Look around your house. Make your list. If you have too many chores, hold some until next time. Chores done regularly will become manageable and not pile up on you!

Types of Chores Possible By Age

Remember, you are the best judge of what your child can handle. The first time you are doing it ***with*** *them- and supervising them after that. You can soon see what they are ready to do.*

Toddler

Help you put away toys and books.

Drop dirty clothes in hamper.

Put away shoes.

Age 3 to 5

Pick up toys.

Put clothes in hamper.

Empty silverware from dishwasher (after you remove sharp knives)

Help you put away their clean clothing

Help put away groceries- putting cans with cans etc.

Age 6 to 8

All of above plus:

Empty dishwasher of items that are kept in lower cabinets

Put away their clean clothing

Place their own dirty dishes in dishwasher after eating

Empty the trashcan in their room into a larger can or bag

Wipe bathroom counter and sink

Help you dust- if you control the furniture polish spray can.

Help carry in groceries and put away.

Wipe baseboards and chair rails with a damp sponge

Age 9 to 11

All of above plus:

Understand what clutter is and know that to tidy a room is to pick up everything that is out of place and return it to its proper home.

Load dishwasher

Dry dishes and put away

Wipe off counter and stovetop

Clean kitchen sink

Collect all the trash around the home and take to the outside can.

Clean the potty

Dust

Clean glass top tables or patio doors with glass cleaner

Vacuum floors

Dry mop (Swiffer®) a hardwood floor

Sweep front walk and porch or back patio

Water houseplants with a small pitcher- make sure to show them how to carefully water so as to not ruin furniture.

Water the garden or outdoor flowers with the hose or sprinkler.

Sweep the floor.

Wipe exterior of appliances.

Rake leaves.

Age 12 – 15

All of above plus:

Handle all of dishwashing chores

Clean the bathtub and/or shower

Shake out rugs.

Mow

Wash and dry throw rugs.

Vacuum stairs

Wet mop a floor

Change sheets

Tidy garage and sweep

Vacuum under the furniture cushions

Wash out trash cans.

Age 16 and up

All of above plus:

Grocery shop

Wipe out refrigerator and discard outdated food

Change AC and heater filter

Chapter 10: Consequences

What Happens When Chores Aren't Done?

"The best laid plans of mice and men often go awry."

Never a truer line than the one adapted from a Robert Burns poem.

You've organized your little heart out.

First there was the determination, the plan, and the action with all of its sorting and purging and storing away properly. Next step is the implementing responsibility and time management techniques.

AND NOW THIS!

"I'm not cleaning this up. You dumped it out!"

"So! You can't make me. Besides, you kicked it over."

"I'm telling on you, you _________!" (Fill in blank with child's favorite word)

"Mom!"

Amid a tumble of blankets and pillows, two grumpy children are surrounded by building blocks, Legos®, shoes, crumpled clean and wrinkled dirty clothing. The Monopoly money is hidden here and there from a pretend robbery gone crazy. The 64-pack of crayons is now an unpopular game of 64-crayon pick-up. Pokémon® cards have tackled baseball cards and no one has won this duel.

"Mom!"

What's a parent to do when two children have turned a room into one big mess?

Believe it or not, Mom and Dad do not have to have the answer to that question.

"They are going to come up with their own ideas," says counselor Susan Fee, an expert on conflict resolution, author of "*My Roommate is Driving Me Crazy*" and a parent.

No matter how organized you are and how much you stress responsibility, you know from experience that the plan will fail at some point, Fee said. Since you know that there will come a day when organization turns to chaos, Fee suggests having a plan in place for dealing with the chaos.

"Ask your children 'How are we going to clean up this when it is really messy," she said. "Empower children with decision. Sit down with them and say that 'We are going to make a plan on how we are going to address this issue.' Listen to their ideas on how to share the clean up or how they should not talk over the top of each other."

Fee suggests that the plan for tackling the room when it becomes messy should be suggested by the children and written down. Give them some time to come up with ideas before suggesting ideas of your own.

Be sure to define what clean means and be very specific.

Fee knows that lesson from her own experience as a parent.

"I say 'Clean your room' and I go back and the bed is not made or better yet, the floor is clean and all the stuff is up on the bed," she said with a chuckle. "You have to come up with your code for clean."

"The fact that they came up with it and wrote it down will keep it fair," she said. "Coming up with your own ideas is very empowering."

At the next disagreement, the parent gets to produce the written plan.

"The mom should say 'Here is the situation and you are both pointing fingers and both screaming it is not fair. This is how we will work through this and resolve this conflict."

Many children are familiar with conflict resolution skills taught at school.

When you produce the plan they have written for cleaning up messes, they are not going to like it, she said.

"This is a test then for the parent. You say 'This is what we have. This is what you agreed to do and this is what we are going to stick to.'" Fee points out that making an agreement and sticking to your word is a life lesson, not a room cleaning lesson.

When the children do make a plan for dealing with a future mess, make sure that they sign the plan.

"You are teaching another life skill. You take things more seriously when you put your name to it," she said.

These kind of contracts can be renegotiated – but not at the time of the clean up. The children came up with the idea, agreed to it and signed their names. They must stick to it. If they are unhappy, they can come up with a new plan AFTER they have cleaned up using the plan they agreed to use.

There should be rewards for a job well done and also consequences for a job not done.

"There is no point in saying 'Calm down,'" Fee said, when two children are arguing. Asking them to calm down and control themselves is possibly something they are not mature enough to do yet. Instead, offer something specific such as "If we can't get this settled in ten minutes, then whatever is left on the floor goes into the donation pile."

But, you really have to donate it. If you do that one or two times, they are going to learn they really have to work things out, she said.

The hard part of being a parent is being consistent. You need consistent rules and consistent response, Fee said.

You are just so not fair!

Sometimes that arguing and conflict is not between siblings. Squabbles about clean-up occur between parent and child and can escalate into a shouting match.

For a parent, this is an opportunity to coach. If stuff is on the floor and children are nasty about how they deal with it then you need to teach them to express what they want, Fee said. Often, she finds they say "he" this or "she" that, casting blame on all things wrong instead of saying what it is they want.

Have specific rules for the children to express their concerns. These rules may include speaking in a calm voice, no name calling, using language that is not attacking and beginning all sentences with "I." Using "I" makes the child say "I want you to," or "I feel angry with" or "I want to."

You'll certainly learn more about what is going on with the "I" rule than listening to a lot of he-said, she-said, and "it's not fair" comments. Discuss these rules with the children, have a consequence if not followed and remind them of the rules when a conflict gets underway.

As a counselor, Fee hears kids say all the time that parents don't listen to them.

"They keep on arguing with you because they have your attention. This is a signal that they are having a time when they feel they are not being heard. If they feel things are not fair, then they do need to be heard. This is where you teach negotiation. You won't get everything you want as a parent and they won't get everything they want as a child but you will find a way to negotiate and a find a way that is fair," Fee said.

Mom-to-Mom Advice

This book is designed as a Mom-to-Mom guide. As one mom to another, I can be honest and tell you that assigning chores and seeing that they are done does not always go smoothly.

Neither does the concept that you are going to do everything yourself, while your child watches television. In that scenario, you are going to eventually become unhappy and frustrated. Realize that any way that you handle family chores, there are bound to be fussing and complaints. It is far better to have the complaints, while they are doing chores, learning to be organized and learning to be responsible than to have complaints and end up doing the chores yourself.

Part of responsibility is learning about consequences. Part of teaching your child to be organized is teaching the consequences. When you sit down and make a family plan with your spouse for handling chores, decide then what the consequences will be if the child does not do the chores.

Don't wait until it happens and come up with lots of threats. Have an action plan.

As an adult, if you don't do your chores, you have consequences. Don't pay the bills on time, you get late fees. Don't shop for groceries; you don't have food in the house. Don't do laundry; you have nothing clean to wear. Don't do your work at your job, you get fired.

What will be your action if the chores don't get done?

In my household, it was rarely an issue if we all did chores at the same time. Everyone else is up and doing their list then it is pretty hard for that one kid to get away with sitting on the sofa. The other family members will see that doesn't happen. The time that it is usually a problem is when you aren't right there to supervise, such as you ask the child to empty the dishwasher or set the table and you don't stand right there.

We had a couple of rules:

1) No fun until the chore was done. No TV. No video games. No computer time. No going outside. If you can't do your work, you can't have fun.

2) What if someone else does your chore? Suppose your child was to tidy the living room before ball practice since

company was arriving later. They leave for ball practice and you discover they did not do the chore and now you jump in and do it. Not only do they miss out on some fun activity when they get home but they should be assigned another chore. Choose something that you need to do and have them do it. Tell them that since you did their chore, they can now do your chore.

To Much to Do and Too Little Time

Here are some additional considerations for dealing with chores and organizing:

> **Are you living in C.h.a.o.s.?**
>
> **C** an't
> **H** ave
> **A** nybody
> **O** ver
> **S** yndrome

Plan for chores:

When you look at your calendar for tomorrow, plan a short time for chores. If everyone gives 15 minutes, you can tidy and keep clutter under control.

Get Real About Too Much Stuff

If you are constantly struggling with stacks and piles of clutter everywhere, then consider that you have too much stuff. Perhaps ***you*** need to make decluttering a priority before tackling a new chore schedule. You can't expect kids to keep things tidy when there is stuff on every surface of the house. Revisit the early chapters on organizing and decluttering. You might need to tackle some organizing projects yourself to get the ball rolling for the family.

Takes time to make time:

Getting organized does take a bit of time but in the long run, you will have much more time if your family is organized.

Tisket a Tasket Use a Basket:

Kids can most certainly help with this chore!

Tackle chaos nightly. This is a chore that can be done by an older child or adult. Grab a laundry basket. Start in the living room. Grab any item that doesn't belong in that room (shoes, hair brush, toy, mail etc) and place in the basket. Go to the next room. Remove any item that belongs in that room. Again, place any item out of place into the basket. Move to the next room and continue in that way until everything has been taken to its home.

***Mom-to-Mom Tip!**

When using the basket technique, I would leave the children's belongings inside their door. It is not up to the person gathering the items to put every person's belongings away.

Think like Bert and Ernie

While humming "which of these things doesn't belong here" you can avoid one of the big mistakes of the disorganized. It is failing to divide. Do you have school paper in one drawer in the kitchen, the construction paper on a shelf in the linen closet, a tub of crayons in the laundry room?

Organizing places like items together. You save time hunting. You save money because you stop buying things that you already own, but just forgot where they were. One of the biggest organizing mistakes is that failure to divide. Object division is the key to teaching our kids to be organized. Divide the items by use. All of the craft items together, the school supply items together, t-shirts together and so on. This is how everything comes to have a home and everything is in its home.

You Can't Wait to Get Organized?

A dose of reality is needed here. Organizing is a living breathing entity. It has to morph, as the kids say. As that baby grows from toddler to school age to preteen, everything changes. How you maintain your home, how your day is organized and how you teach them will change. What they can and cannot do for themselves will change. We certainly hope so! We have that perpetual hope that they will eventually be potty trained, make their own bed, and put their own dishes in the dishwasher and so on.

Along the way, don't make the biggest mistake of the disorganized. Don't ever get in the rut of the "I've always done it this way." Be prepared to change as needed and be prepared to anticipate change.

When a system of planning your day or organizing some aspect of your life stops working, then find a new way. This is how you must teach your children. They will get a task down pat, such as packing their own backpack, and all of a sudden they are playing sports and now also need to pack a snack for after school and sports equipment. It adds a new level to getting ready. Instead of taking over for them, you will be helping them adapt to a new routine. Change is inevitable.

Yes, you can get organized - and if you do a good job, you will get organized over and over and over.

Mission Disorganized

If you want to get organized, one of the mistakes you need to pitch out before it happens are those unrealistic expectations. As much fun as *TLC's Clean Sweep* and *HGTV's Mission Organization* are to watch, they are just TV shows. You have real life and if you are like most moms, your real life does not come with an interior decorator, carpenter, and lots of worker bees to carry things in and out. In the back of your mind you realize that, I am sure, but in the front of your mind, you are thinking that you ought to be able to perform some kind of miracle in an hour or less.

Be good to yourself. Be good to your kids. Adopt a good enough is grand attitude. It's wonderful to be able to shout "Great," or "Terrific" as everything lines up in perfect order. But a family is made of people and people are not perfect. ***If your son makes it downstairs in time, dressed properly, holding his backpack with everything in it***, packed by himself, and reminds YOU that he has something after school and that he already packed his own snack then shout "Terrific" and when you wonder upstairs later and find a wet towel on the floor change the shout to "Good Enough" and think that good enough is grand.

Focus on the whole. Look for a lot of steps done right rather than the misstep along the way. Good enough is indeed grand!

Chapter 11: Time Management

Morning Launch Pad

Getting Off To an Organized Start

If rocket ships launch on a fuel of hot air, I bet yours would be moon bound by now. I know that mine would.

Yelling, up the stairs or down the hall, has been everyone's routine at some point.

"Don't forget your soccer cleats!"

"What did you do with that permission slip?"

"Do you have that check for lunch money?"

"Isn't today library day for your class? Get your book!"

This is a VERY effective method if you intend to be your child's personal organizer from now until they leave for college. Not only do they not have to remember anything themselves but conveniently, they can blame you for missing items.

"Mom! You got me in trouble. You didn't tell me it was library day!"

Once again, as parents, we have to be careful not to push our child off the high dive of responsibility. We go along being their personal reminder service until one day something snaps and we growl at them that they must keep up with their own stuff from now on.

"Don't be calling me at work, mister," you fuss. "From now on you are own your own to remember those PE clothes." That is pushing your child off the high dive. You've gone from doing it for them to having them do it with no coaching in-between. Let's shoot for some middle ground between you pushing them off that high dive and you reminding them of every little thing.

This is where that launch pad comes in.

Just like a rocket ship requires a launch pad, so does your family. It is a designated staging area where the family prepares to launch out for the day. The night before, everything that must go out the door, goes into the launch pad. Adults also benefit by a launch pad. You should have a place for everything you need as well, from that briefcase to car keys to items that must be returned to the store.

One of the very best tools for teaching organization is a small wipe-off board. You can even find them at dollar-type stores. Each child should have and use one.

The wipe-off board is a key part to the launch pad. It might be kept at the launch pad or perhaps on the child's bedroom door. Each item that is needed for the next day, both for school and after-school activities, is listed on the wipe-off board. You should not do this for your child but you should supervise them making the list. Encourage them to think of everything that should be on the list. You are teaching both organization and personal responsibility.

*Mom-to-Mom Tip!

You can begin to use the wipe-off board with your 4 and 5 year old non-readers. Draw a picture of a book, a sweater and so forth. They can learn to pack the things.

Once the child has listed everything, the wipe-off board is your new parenting best friend. Instead of being that personal organizer, you are teaching your child to be their own organizer. You will still need to remind them – and probably daily- but the reminding is different in nature.

"Do you have everything on your list?"

That will be your question. You are still reminding. You are still supervising but you have placed the burden of responsibility on them. They are learning to think in an organized manner, plan ahead and check their own list. All of these are valuable skills. Down the road, as they are older, they will no longer need you to remind them.

The Growing Pains of Time Management

One day, I was working on a tight deadline and my cell phone rang. My dramatic daughter issued a suffering sigh and announced "Mom, you HAVE got to come to school with my soccer cleats or I am going to have to run laps."

I quickly mulled this over in my head. Over time, I had delivered keys, notes, papers, PE clothing and more. Apparently delivery was in my mommy job description?

Today, it meant abandoning my project, which was progressing along nicely toward today's deadline, and returning to it later. It meant a 20 minute drive home to get the cleats then a 20 minute drive to school, then a 20 minute drive back to work. After losing an hour of my work day, I'd be hard pressed to make that deadline before having to return back to school to pick up the same child.

"I'm sorry but I can't do that," I said.

Following my answer was a terse and unpleasant exchange but I stuck to my guns.

Guess what? I got to school to pick her up and she was still alive. She had survived running a few laps.

During my drive to pick her up, I reflected that the mommy delivery service was a product of my own making. I felt sorry for them- each time- and aimed to please. The fact of the matter is that the college professor isn't going to feel sorry for their tardiness. Their boss isn't going to forgive it. It is a habit that should not be developed.

So alongside the launch pad and wipe-off board, establish some family rules concerning the responsibility of forgotten items.

In my household, I learned to give them two chances. After all, we are human and what adult hasn't forgotten something? I told them that twice during the school year I would bring them the missing item- if at all possible. Other times, they'd have to suffer the consequences.

Not too long after that, my other daughter called with a momentary crisis. She wanted some item brought to her that she had forgotten.

"I can do that," I said. "But, remember you only have two chances this school year. Do you want to use one on this?"

She paused and then said "Never mind. It is not that big of a deal. I'll be fine."

And so she was.

*Mom-to-Mom Tip!

Establish a **launch pad** near the door your family uses. Create a way to hold items for each member of the **family**. This may be hooks, shelves or possibly bins in a rack on wheels. **Think** of a way that works with your home.

*Mom-to-Mom Tip!

If you live in an apartment or a very small home, you use your dining area as a launch pad. Book bags can be hung from the back of chairs. If you are clever with a needle and thread, you can sew a cover for the back of the chair that has a pocket for each person to drop in their items for the next day.

- Place packed book bags, jackets, library books etc on the launch pad each evening.
- Mom and Dad should have a pad too and use it for purses, briefcase, keys etc.

*Mom-to-Mom Tip!

Personal responsibility is not just what is in the backpack but accepting responsibility for your choices or the errors that you might make along the way. In a world where too many kids think everything is someone else's fault, it's a pretty powerful lesson.

*Mom-to-Mom Tip!

Getting organized is a great way to avoid a constant mess at the door. If you have shelves, baskets or hooks, then it should be easier to be neat and harder to be messy.

Bathroom Launch Tips

Another problem area for kids is the bathroom. They are sent off to brush their teeth or wash their face so that you can get out the door. Next thing you know, they are dawdling and you are yelling for them to hurry or they have returned to the kitchen but still are not entirely ready to leave. Here are some tips to help with the bathroom:

Have a mini-launch pad in the bathroom. Give each person a drawer, shelf or caddy. Put their name on it.

Let each person have his or her own supplies. Nothing can make two kids argue like only having one tube of toothpaste!

Add an easy to read clock. Part of the problem in the bathroom is that no one ever knows the time. You can enhance the clock by adding a small red dot or an arrow to the clock face showing the time that they must leave the house for school.

Some children are sleepy-heads. They simply can't remember to brush their teeth AND wash their face AND comb their hair etc. **Add a checklist** for children that need one so that you don't have to keep asking them if they did this or that. Instead, send them back to check their list.

*Mom-to-Mom Tip!

Young children will get lessons on telling time at school. Continue to work on that at home. They can't very well know if they are running late if they can't even tell time! Wearing a watch is a great habit to begin. One with an alarm setting can be handy. For example, if they are allowed to play outside for an hour before beginning homework, have them set the watch alarm. Again, it is teaching personal responsibility and time management.

Other Great Launch Tips

Shop with a color scheme for clothing. If shopping for a younger child, choose easy to mix and match pieces. Read the labels and pick those that easily machine wash and dry. Try purchasing only solid color bottoms and a variety of printed or solid shirts so that pretty much anything they put together will match.

Lay out clothing the night before, including school uniforms. Sometimes, uniforms are deceiving to our mental planning. We think we have the dressing issue covered because the child wears uniforms. But, it can only make a problem more frantic as there aren't a lot of back-up choices when a shirt has a mustard stain or the pants are still wet in the dryer.

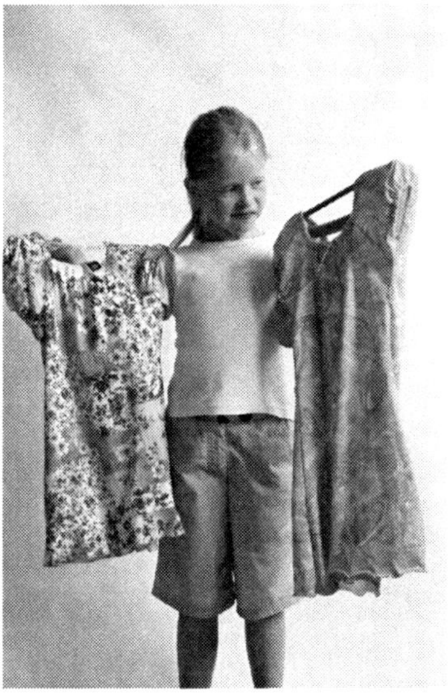

*Mom-to-Mom Tip!

Create a school week organizer. In your child's closet, add some shelves that hang from the closet bar. You buy ones that are sold as a sweater keeper or accessory organizer. In some stores, you can actually find school day organizers already labeled with the day of the week. Any product that offers five days of shelving will work fine.

On Sunday evening, have the child choose five outfits for the week, complete with socks and undies. The outfits are placed in the organizer. The next morning, no battle over what to wear. They have five clean outfits lined up and can choose any of them.

This is an especially good tip for older girls. By that time, most of their clothing will be on hangers. Create a launch area in the closet. Have them choose five outfits and hang them together in the closet. There will be much less morning stress – for you and for them.

Create a breakfast menu. Very often, parents are constantly repeating the menu as if they were at a fast food restaurant window. Daily, do you ask if they want waffles, a bagel, and oatmeal and so on? Repeating daily and for each child? After grocery shopping, use a wipe-off board on the fridge for a menu. After all, kids love ordering off a menu. List the items that are in the house for breakfast. No more conversations where you list everything and they whine that they don't want those things and you beg them to eat something. Put up the list. Develop personal responsibility. They can read it and choose and you can move on to another task besides reciting today's specials.

Use sticky notes for reminders. Need to remember to take juice to school? Add a sticky note to the backpack.

*Mom-to-Mom Tip!

Sticky notes are the parent's friend. Not only should you encourage the child to leave a note for themselves but you should use them. Stick them to doors and mirrors and clocks or backpacks…anywhere they will be seen. As a parent, using a sticky note can often alleviate a verbal tussle that might happen with a voiced reminder.

Evening's Safe Landing

Or, how to avoid a refrigerator full of food and nothing to serve

Make a menu and shop with a list for a full week's worth of meals.
Have kids contribute menu ideas.

Develop menus around your calendar. Check to see which nights are too busy and need a quicker meal and which night you might be able to double the recipe.

For busy nights:

Make use of the Crock-Pot, make-ahead casseroles or one-dish meals.

Make two and freeze one at least once a week.

Get in a habit of checking tomorrow night's dinner ingredients tonight. Make the casserole, salad, or drop it in the Crock-Pot the night before or early morning. Thaw the meat.

Keep and recycle the menus.

Invite the children to help you prepare dinner. They can recite spelling words or be quizzed for a test while they chop a green pepper or tear up lettuce for a salad.

Just for Fun!

Here are a couple of kid friendly recipes that are time friendly for mom. They are both so simple that an older child, about 4th grade on up, can handle them as well.

Shredded Beef Sandwiches Au Jus

* *Below is a recipe for beef sandwiches served au jus. The beef has a great flavor and the vinegar makes it very tender. I serve it on hoagie rolls but if you have some leftover and want a different meal, use it to top rice or noodles. Serve it at parties with smaller, dinner sized rolls for a hot finger-food size sandwich.*

3-pound beef chuck pot roast
1/3-cup vinegar (this seems like too little liquid but it works great!)
1 large onion, diced
3 bay leaves
½ t. salt
¼ t. garlic powder
8-10 French Sub Rolls

Trim fat from roast. Place in a Crock Pot. Combine remaining ingredients, except rolls, and pour over roast. Cook on low 10 to 12 hours. Using two forks, shred meat, pushing down into juices. The meat is so tender this only takes a minute. Discard any fat or bones. Serve on rolls with a tiny side dish of au jus for dipping.

Busy Mom's Tip: Round out the nutrition by serving with bagged Cole slaw topped with bottled dressing and a mug of tomato soup.

Quick Vegetable Soup

1-pound ground beef
1 can pinto beans
1 can Ro*tel®
3 cans tomato soup
4 cans Veg•All®

Brown the beef in a soup pot; drain off fat. Add remaining ingredients. Bring to a boil, reduce to simmer and serve.

A Busy Mom's Tip: It is so easy to brown meat in the microwave. Then, you can just slip the dishes into the dishwasher. Here's how!
Place the ground beef in a plastic colander. Set the calendar inside a microwave-safe bowl. Break the beef up with a fork. Microwave for 2 minutes and break the beef up again. Repeat at 2 minutes intervals until beef is no longer pink. Discard fat that has drained into the bowl.

An Organizing Day Dinner!
Easy Chicken Nachos

3 chicken breasts
1 can beans- black or pinto, drained
1 can corn, drained
1 cup salsa
Shredded cheddar

Place breasts, beans, corn and salsa in Crock-Pot. Cook on low 4 hours while organizing. Use two forks to shred cooked chicken. Top with cheese. Scoop up with chips, roll in soft-shell tortillas or top a bed of lettuce and tomato for a hot salad.

Chapter 12: Organizing Homework

Creating homework rituals

Creating Homework rituals
for <u>time</u> and <u>place</u>
creates good habits.

- ***Create a homework area***. This might be a desk. It might be the kitchen table. It will probably change as they grow. The important considerations are these. Have it be in a set spot. Choose a location that limits distractions but not so hidden that you can't supervise.

- ***For the desk:*** Add a good light, a holder for pens,

pencils, markers and the like. I like to see it be a happy place. A bulletin board over the desk can showcase art work or papers where the child has done well or shown improvement. This sets up a positive environment. You want it to be bright, fun and comfortable yet not distracting so move toys, games and distractions off of the desktop.

- ***For the kitchen table:*** Young ones often do best at the kitchen table because running back and forth to find you, with their many questions, takes a great deal of time and creates lengthy distractions. You continue to have to refocus them back to the task at hand. Create a portable work center for the table. Choose a container that can be

placed on the table each day at homework time. It could be a basket, box or other container you have in the house. Add some cups to it to hold pens, pencils, markers, and colored pencils. Add scissors, tape, glue stick, notebook paper and any special items your child might use regularly, such as index cards or graph paper. Each day, part of the homework ritual will be to transform the table to a homework station by placing the container of supplies on the table and clearing off any toys or other distractions.

One of the frustrations of homework always seems to come on an especially busy day. Your child suddenly informs you that they need a poster for tomorrow or they got in trouble for not having paper and had to borrow paper from someone. You find yourself racing out to the nearest store. Even a quick trip can be another 30 minutes you didn't need to waste. Save time for yourself by making a school supply center within your home. Choose a shelf in a closet or even a plastic tub. Buy multiples of the things on your child's school supply list- pencils, packs of paper, ruler and so forth. Include those seldom-used supplies you have to run out and get such as poster boards, report covers, glue sticks and construction paper.

Checklist for Stocking up on School Supplies

Paper
Pens
Pencils
Erasers
Pencil sharpener
Extra-lead for mechanical pencils
Crayons
Markers
Highlighters
Colored Pencils
Glue and/or glue stick
3-hole punch
1-hole punch
Adhesive hole reinforcements (to repair hole rips)
Stapler
Staples
Calculator
Spell checker
Index cards
Dictionary
Thesaurus
Paper Clips
Sticky notes
Scissors
Ruler

*Mom-to-Mom Tip!

Label all of your child's supplies, even individual markers and crayons. It only takes a minute and saves you from running to the store to replace "lost" supplies.

Have a *set time* for homework. Before you panic at that statement, keep reading. I realize that you have a busy schedule and that is why you are reading this book.

There are two ways to have a set time for homework. Part of the frustration in school day parenting is getting that homework done. We all dread the days when it draws late and the child is tired and we are tired and yet homework remains to be done. Avoid this frustration by having that set time for homework in <u>one of these two ways</u>.

1) If you are lucky enough to have a steady daily schedule, then have a set time, such as 5 o'clock daily. Part of learning to be organized is learning to have a routine and not rush around everyday like a chicken with her head cut-off. Having a set time means you can end the constant negotiation with your child when they want to put off and put off the inevitable.

2) For those whose schedule changes every day, a *set time* means looking at the calendar and setting a time for the following day. There may be many variables in your family life. You may have a job with shifting hours. You may have several children with activities and practices or religious studies. It might be impossible for you to dictate that homework is at the same time daily. Instead, having a set time means that each night you will look at the calendar for the next day. Based on that child's day, the two of you will then pick a homework time for tomorrow and that time will vary daily. You are imparting an important lesson here. ***Time management means always prioritizing and knowing what needs to be done when.***

You are teaching your child how to manage their time well. You are showing them that despite activities or sports, you are always putting education first by planning for it rather than leaving the most important part of their day to chance. When the day comes that you and the child study tomorrow's calendar (which you should be doing together daily following that day's homework) and neither of you can figure out when homework will get done tomorrow, then you have a problem. It is important to address that problem rather then assume it will work itself out. If your life and child's life is so busy that neither of you can' figure out when to do homework, obviously you have to make changes, and fast. You will find more information on time management in the calendar section of this book.

Long Term Projects

For those long projects, such a paper that needs to be written, book reports, science projects and the like, organization and planning is important. It is not just for your child to be successful but for household peace. How many parents have been driven crazy by late nights and last minute rushing over school projects?

*Mom-to-Mom Tip!

Even adults forget what time they have to be places. Keep a stack of index cards by the calendar. Make it a routine to look at the calendar with your child. Have them note on the index card the time for tomorrow's practice or meetings as well as the homework time. Tuck the car into the backpack.

Some teachers are helpful in organizing a project. They may ask for a topic idea on one date, an outline on another date and a rough draft on another date. They are trying to teach the child to pace the project. But, even with those deadlines, there are multiple steps to meeting the deadlines. As you read below, you will see that there are a huge number of steps in a project and you can see why it typically doesn't work for a parent to just keep saying "You need to work on that!"

You Know You're Disorganized if...

Your child used to blame the dog, but now, tells the teacher his parents lost his homework!

Here are some tips for dealing with long term projects. Remember, all along the way, you are teaching organizational and planning skills. You are guiding and directing but not doing it for them. When your student announces they have a project coming up, try these:

- Have child make a written list of the steps needed. You will probably need to ask them a number of questions as you walk them through the steps as they think about what they have to do. This is all part of the process of teaching them personal responsibility and how to be organized. For example, using a typical science leaf collection task, project steps might include: going to the library for a leaf identification book, going outdoors to woods to collect and label the leaves, going to the office supply store for materials, mounting and labeling the leaves, doing research on each tree on the Internet or encyclopedia, writing a paragraph or listing information about each tree and assembling the final project.

- Teach them to place the steps on the calendar by working backward from the due date. Find the due date on the calendar. Plan for it to be done a few days early. Now work to place all of the steps for the project on the calendar. Some steps might take more than one time. For example, it might take you two trips to collect leaves or two sessions to mount the leaves and four sessions to look them up on-line.
- Planning ahead like this relieves a lot of stress for both the child and parent. You don't have to continually nag and guess if they have done enough of the project to be ready on time. Instead, you will be able to compare what they have done to the plan on the calendar and know if they are on track or not. You have taught them a great lesson in planning for the many future projects and they will carry this into college and the workplace.

Short-term projects

These are the ones that the teacher might give on a Monday ask for it to be done by Friday. Use the same plan as above. Make a list of tasks and look at week's activities. Divide up on calendar so that some work is done each day.

Reading Assignments

When football, shooting hoops, playing in the snow and video games all pull on them after school, it is hard sometimes to get them to sit and read. We used to struggle with reading time. I set a timer and asked my son to read 10 minutes or five more pages. It was always a negotiation and sometimes, since the brain would drift away, those 10 minutes of reading might equal an actual two minutes of reading. Too soon, the teacher would be expecting them to take a test on a book not finished. To solve that, we came up with these more organized ideas for reading of school work.

- If your child has to read so much in a given week, make bookmarkers labeled with the days of the week. Or, if it is a longer time frame, for an older child reading a novel, then use dates….such as Oct. 10, Oct. 12 and so forth.
- Divide the book with the markers; placing them so that is spreads out the reading so that it will be finished on time.
- Have the child read to the next marker – it eliminates arguing and negotiation and teaches them how to pace out a project. This division of reading assignments will help them in both high school and college.

Chapter 13: Paperwork Organization

Getting Paper Control!

All you need for paper control are more refrigerator magnets! Right?

Well, of course the refrigerator door is the perfect system for handling all of our important papers to keep and our to-do lists! When there aren't enough refrigerator magnets in the world to help you, it's time to get serious about organizing kids' papers.

Organizing Piles and Piles of Children's Papers

What is a must have storage item that parents cannot live without?

A filing cabinet or crate!

Parents struggle with corralling school papers, projects, notes the child has taken, notes from the teacher, assignment directions, syllabi, supply lists, spelling lists, reading lists and calendars.

Filing paperwork, a learned skill, is an important life-long habit that will help establish success from the middle school years well into the workforce. It is so easy to begin this in the early grades and create a habit.

Invest in a lightweight, inexpensive file crate. File crates, found in office supply and department stores, are sometimes called milk crates. They have rims to hold colorful hanging file folders. File crates, folders and labels come in many bright fun colors that your kids could help choose.

> **Filing paperwork, a learned skill, is an important life-long habit that will help establish success from the middle school years well into the workforce.**

For the younger children, teach them how to make a folder for each month. They might want to decorate the folders. For the older student, have them make a file for each subject and plus a folder for notes/calendars from school.

How to Teach Paper Management

Each day, look at their work. Supervise the children unpacking their backpacks into the correct folder. This is teaching a lifelong skill that everything has its place – even papers! It eliminates Mom and Dad from drowning in a sea of papers. For the older children, they will accumulate all the materials they need for reviews and exams in one area. Being organized is one key to success in school.

*Mom-to-Mom Tip!

At the end of the year, start a fun new tradition. After you have selected some treasured papers and art work to keep, have an end-of-the-year barbecue. Celebrate moving on to a new grade by toasting marshmallows and making s'mores over the burning of the old homework papers! The kids will love it!

Follow this Step-By-Step to Organize Kids' Papers

Purchase a large file box or file crate. They come in many colors!

Purchase hanging file folders. They come in many colors!

For younger children:

Help them create files for the months of the year.

Teach them to put their papers in the file each night.

At year-end, bundle all or bundle a few, off to the attic.

Create new files for the new school year.

For older students:

Teach them how-to create files for each subject.

Have them keep all the papers in the file.

Encourage building this habit, as it is an important life tool.

As soon as possible, begin to teach financial responsibility.

Have them create files for their bank statements, bills and even for taxes from part-time jobs.

*Mom-to-Mom Tip!

At the year end, sort through the papers and choose some favorites that represent the year. Store those in plastic boxes in the attic or the top of the closet. A clean, new pizza box makes a nice container for storing art work. Ask for a new clean one from your favorite pizza

"But Mom, How can I be out of Money," the college freshman cried. "I've still got some checks in my checkbook."

*Mom-to-Mom Tip!

As your child enters high school, it is time for them to keep track of their own bank statements, debit cards, cell phone bills and allowance. Make sure you don't just hand the chore to them. Take the time to show them how to balance a bank statement, how to file and how to keep track of when their bills are due. Trust me, when they get in college and you get phone calls home for more money, you'll wish you had done this.

Even better, deposit funds into their own checking account and make them responsible for paying that cell bill or the insurance bill on their car. If they are old enough to drive, they are old enough to write a check and mail a bill (and you will of course check!)

Chapter 14: Organizing Brain Cells

Jogging the Memory: Organizing with Lists

Teach your kids the habit of making lists. List making is an important part of being organized. It encompasses time management and responsibility. Here are a few ways to use lists- and teach your child to use lists.

In your launch pad area, have your child use a wipe-off board(s) to list and check off these items.

- Chores
- Things to do
- Packing list for school
  - Assist the list maker but don't make the list yourself.
  - Check behind them to make sure the list is correct.

- For non-readers, draw the item to be remembered.
- Don't remind the child to find an item. Instead, do remind the child, often, to check their list.

Organizing with Calendars

Make using a calendar a habit for your child.

Begin by teaching children to help you add activities to your calendar. Let them find the day and the month but you write on the calendar. For elementary age and older, they can discuss it with you so you are aware what is being added to the calendar, but have them do the actual writing.

Make a nightly ritual to check the family calendar. Have the child find tomorrows' date and read the calendar out loud to you.

Have older children, keep their own calendar. Each night they should check it and discuss tomorrow's activities with you. You will want to keep their dates on your calendar as well. Why keep two calendars when you could just do it yourself? You are trying to develop responsibility in your child. They need to learn to keep track of where they need to be and when….and keep you apprised of it.

Reinforce their calendar habit. Ask often what they have on their calendar for the day.

*Mom-to-Mom Tip!

A gigantic family calendar can certainly be helpful in getting everyone where they need to be. However, remember that if you are the only one checking it and writing on it, you haven't taught your children anything about being responsible with their time or planning. A wipe-off one on the fridge would be great!

Chapter 15: Organizing Laundry

Wash Out the Wazoo

I don't know where exactly the wazoo is located. However, I do know that I frequently said we had laundry out the wazoo. What do you do when you are in laundry room overload and the kids just seem to bring on more and more wash?

You get busy and get organized!!!!

Stop Kiddie

Washer to Hamper Overload

Now is the perfect time for your child to do his or her laundry.

I am dead serious so stop laughing. Our young children can microwave mac and cheese, look up stuff on the Internet all while finding the secret passages on the latest video game. My point to this, you ask? They can push full load, warm water and add soap to the machine.

This lightening bolt stuck me smack in the lower back as I scooped up another heap of once neatly folded clean laundry off the floor. It had resided on the end of the bed prior to my carting it to the laundry, sorting, pre-treating, washing, drying, folding and returning to beloved child's room like a magic wand had been waved. Presumably it was too much to expect them to put it in the drawer.

The straw that broke the proverbial camel's back came when, after demanding that rooms be cleaned immediately, I found partially folded, rumpled "clean" laundry in the smelly hamper. Obviously it was easier to return it to the parental laundry machine than to put it in the drawer. For me, that was the great motivation to come up with a new family laundry routine!

Of course, like every lesson, we demonstrate and supervise. When my children left elementary school, I stopped doing all the family laundry. I used to go room-to-room, gathering, sorting and later distributing laundry. Instead, we began a designated laundry day per child.

The child gathered. Together, we read labels, soapboxes and machine dials. Admittedly I learned a few things as well - lots of info on those soap boxes that I had never taken the time to read. We sorted. The child pretreated, washed, dried, folded and put away while I watched.

Organizing is not just a matter of having a place for things and things in their place. You need time to be organized. Three kids, two schools, four sports teams, one full-time job and one Girl Scout troupe meant my children had more time to fold their laundry than I did. I was trying to handle the laundry of five and they only had one.

When my children became responsible for their own clothing it stopped the clean wardrobe from being tossed on the floor. Amazingly, they were willing to hang something up and, horrors, wear it twice before washing.

Actually, this was a really easy lesson. I taught the lesson and made it a family rule and that was that. After a period of supervision, then came a period where I just reminded them it was their laundry night. Later, I stopped reminding them. Since they seemed to always remember the exact day, minute and channel of their favorite TV show, they could remember to wash.

Punishment was self-inflected. In other words if they had nothing clean to wear, it was their own fault. It happened a few times and they had to go to school in clothes from their hamper.

Organization isn't a talent. It's a taught skill. Teaching your children self-responsibility teaches them to be organized and their household help grants you more time to organize yourself.

I haven't done my kids' laundry in a few years, and by the way, they still love me.

Laundry Step-by-Step

Here are some ideas of tasks your child might be able to accomplish. These are all tasks that you would do anyway. The difference is that you are doing them with your child instead of FOR your child.

The Toddler

Your child can begin to do laundry when they are a toddler. This is where you begin to teach them that first family rule: Everything has a place. After each bath, take them to the hamper with you. Drop in a piece of clothing and praise them. Then give them a piece to drop in the hamper. Clap and praise them. Make putting the clothes in the hamper a nightly fun ritual.

Ages Three to Five

In addition to putting clothes in the hamper, they can begin to do more related chores.

They can return towel to the bathroom; placing it on the side of the tub- they can easily reach the tub. You can hang it up for them.

When they are taller, they can use a step-stool to place it on a towel bar or add a lower towel bar to the back of the bathroom door for the tykes to use. The way they hang the towel might not be neat but the lesson is personal responsibility and that everything has a home.

Place picture labels on the dresser drawer. Make sorting the clean laundry a game. Have them find the sock picture and then help put the socks from the basket to the drawer. Repeat with the other items.

Ages Six and Seven

Children this age love to be helpers. Capitalize on that. Have children help you gather dirty clothes and take to the washer. They can help you sort clothes into light and dark piles. Sometimes this is hard even for adults but they generally will have a good time making decisions if it is light or dark- or for example, finding all the red items.

Let them squirt. Kids love to squirt. Have them help hunt for the stains and allow them to squirt them with the stain remover. You can spread a soiled towel on the floor to give them an area to place the dirty item and squirt under your supervision.

They can also remove items from the dryer.

Ages Eight to Ten

Working under your supervision, in addition to all of the above, expect that:

:

They can read the tags inside the clothing for special washing instructions.

They can read the soap box for instructions.

They can place the sorted clothing in the washer.

They can measure and add soap.

They can move the wet clothing to the dryer.

They can add a dryer fabric softener to the dryer.

They can select the temperature and press start.

Again, remember that for safety sake, all of the above is under your supervision.

They can fold a good deal of the laundry. They should be able to match and fold socks. They can fold other items that won't be harmed if they get a bit wrinkled, such as underwear and pajamas while you fold the rest.

Age 11 through Middle School

At this point, they should be entering or in Middle School. Remember now, they have been operating a computer and a microwave and other items for quite a few years. They should be able to operate a washer and dryer since you have taken the time to show them. By Middle School, a child should:

Be able to fold all of their laundry or place it on hangers. The only exception is special or dressy clothing that may need mom's ironing.

Place their own clothing in the hamper.

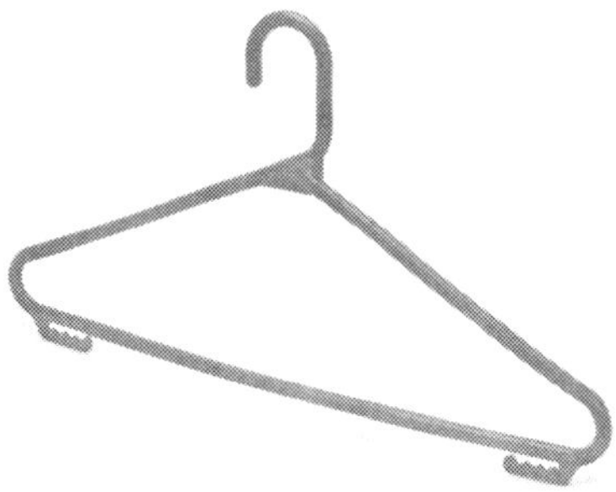

Take the clothing to the laundry room.

Sort it into lights and darks.

Squirt it with stain treatment.

Place it in the washer and press the correct buttons.

Transfer it to the dryer and press the correct buttons.

Fold or hang their clothing.

Place the clean clothing away where it belongs.

High School Years

Now is the time to add that last step – ironing. Most of our clothing no longer needs ironing but there is always that shirt for a job interview or that dress for a special occasion. Everyone should know how to get out a few wrinkles.

As occasions arise for ironing, don't do it for them. Do it with them.

- Have them check the label for fabric content.
- Have them compare it to the iron's fabric settings to choose the correct one.
- Demonstrate on a small area and then let them give it a try.
- Go over safety instructions for handling the hot iron, turning it off and keeping it unplugged.
- Consider using a t-shirt for your ironing lesson then move on to the real wrinkled garment.

Chapter 16: Kitchen Capers

Keeping the Kitchen Fun and Calm

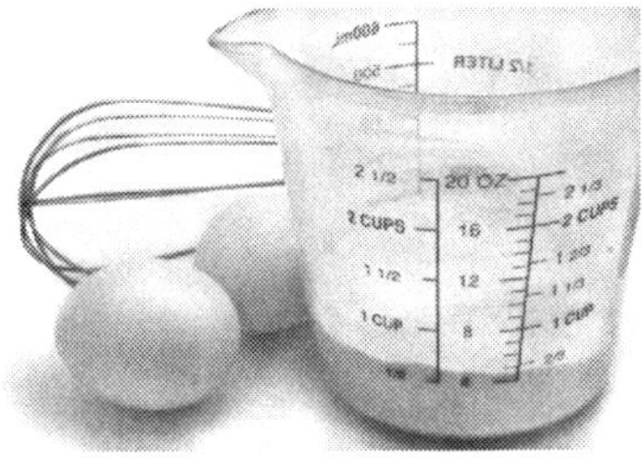

Ten Minutes of Peace, Please

"Please Lord, just ten minutes of peace and quiet," I whispered softly to myself.

Closing the door on my sleeping husband, I tiptoed down the hall.

Since I was due any day now with child number two, I could really use those ten minutes and cup of coffee, decaf of course. I could then deal with a day only the mother of an almost two-year old can imagine.

It's no wonder I was tired. When I gave up on sleeping last night, I got up and cleaned house. I tidied cabinets, polished appliances and scrubbed the floor of the kitchen. Since I could barely tie my shoes, the last chore was a miracle. There is no doubt that I was "nesting" on this day. Not only was I looking forward to that cup of coffee but I was looking forward to sitting in my newly cleaned space.

I mean how long does any clean surface last with a toddler?

I shuffled into the kitchen and nearly screamed. My tiny kitchen, with its gleaming celery green countertops and white appliances was splattered with bright orange.

Orange drips ran down the face of the cabinets and oozed onto the floor. Neon orange designs were in puddles here and there. The white refrigerator door was sticky with goop.

My brain could not even make sense what it was seeing. How in the world could a room be sparkling clean at 3 a.m. and look like an orange soda explosion at 7 a.m.?

Lowering myself to a kitchen chair, I soon realized that all of the mess didn't go higher than two and half feet high. Only one short person lives here.

"But, he can't even open the refrigerator," I thought.

Opening the fridge, I found the source of the orange explosion. On the bottom shelf of the fridge, the plastic wrap had been removed from a bowl of orange gelatin. In the gelatin, I could see the tiny handprints of the culprit. It was obvious that he *could* open the fridge.

As I headed down the hall, I could see blobs of melted gelatin nestled in the carpeting. The trail led me right to my son's room.

Cracking open the door softly, I crept up to his bed. Nestled under a comforter decorated with cars and trucks snoozed a little blond-haired angel. The morning sun streamed in on him.

Only today, this angel had an orange moustache that went from ear to ear. His two hands were as orange as a Jack-O-Lantern. Next to his bed, the morning sun also streamed in on two former piles of gelatin on his dresser. They were now melting and running down the front of a family heirloom.

I sat down on the end of the bed with a sigh and watched the orange angel sleep. He'd made a devil of a mess and for the life of me I couldn't figure out why, or when.

Pretty soon, the sun was bright and he woke with a grin, tickled that Mommy was sitting on his bed.

"I see that you've had breakfast," I said.

Screwing up his button nose, he frowned and said "No. I hungry."

Scooping him up, I headed down the hall toward the kitchen, stopping first at the bathroom mirror. He greeted his little orange face with a burst of giggles.

Heading back down the hall, I set him down in the kitchen and his eyes got round at the orange mess.

"I fix it," he says with a nod. He then tried in vain to reach a towel.

"Why didn't you get a bowl," I questioned.

Silly me! The moment I opened my mouth, I knew the answer. He could not reach a bowl or plate or cup. He could not reach a towel or paper towel.

Opening the fridge, I studied the contents. Jars of salad dressing and mayonnaise paraded in the door. Raw vegetables lined the bins. The gallon jugs of juice and milk, too heavy for a child, were out of reach on the top shelf. The cabinets of other foods were out of reach as well.

I'd created the most perfect child-proof and equally child un-friendly kitchen possible.

"You poor kid," I said, snuggling him close and smelling the sweaty little boy smell mingled with citrus. "I bet you really were hungry."

Organize the Kitchen for the Kids

- Kitchen Cabinet: Choose a lower cabinet and empty it. Into it, place all of the kid-friendly dishes. Put in it the plastic Spiderman bowl, Barbie plate and sippee cups. Add a container to hold the child-size flatware. Put in a napkin holder with napkins. Not only can they set their place at the table and get a cup when they want a drink but they can help empty the dishwasher and put their own clean dishes away.

Little ones enjoy water play and rinsing their dishes is just that!

- Pantry: If you have young children and there are some things you do not want to them to constantly help themselves to, then you might place the snacks on an adult-height shelf. Take a clear box and place an assortment of approved children's snacks, such as granola bars, at a lower level for them. Likewise, if your children pack their lunches choose a lower shelf and place all the items that they may take in their lunchbox.
- Refrigerator: Have a snack zone in the fridge. Add a bowl of fruit that everyone likes, such as grapes or oranges. Add your small vegetable nibbles, containers of yogurt or pudding, cheese sticks and so on. This keeps everyone from rummaging through the fridge and also keeps them from eating ingredients you have planned to use in meals.

Lunch Packing Lessons

One child is yelling about missing PE clothes and another shouting that their life is over because their hair is standing up. In between those issues, breakfast and the normal chaos, is dealing with packing lunches which can be the proverbial straw that broke the camel's back.

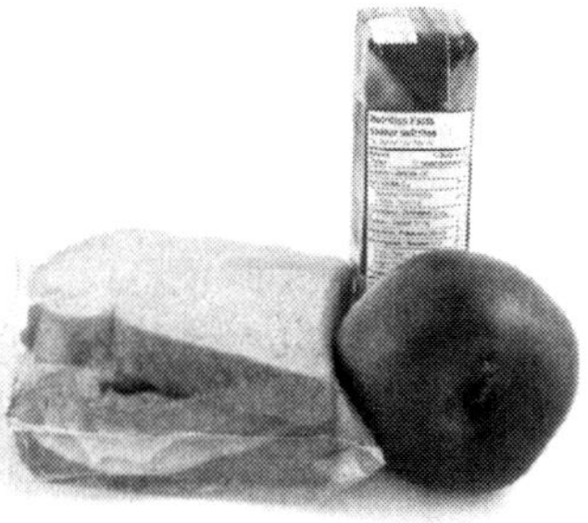

Getting organized to deal with school lunches is certainly worth the small amount of time involved.

Our kitchens, when set up to function properly, have a certain layout and rhythm. Most likely, I'd find the coffee and coffee filters near the coffee pot at your house. The things for baking are all together. Your cookware, pots and pans, are surely near the stove.

Yet, when it comes to lunch making, I bet you have to go to one drawer for plastic bags, another for a paper bag and then another drawer for a plastic fork or spoon. You grab a napkin from the napkin holder, peanut butter one cabinet and a small bag of chips from another. Multiply that times several children!

To be honest, you are lucky if there is a bag of chips or container of pudding. Most likely, family members stay confused about what is okay for snacking and what is off limits. Now you are grumpy and in a rush to try to find something else to put in the lunch.

Somehow, when you were not looking, someone snacked on all the individually packaged lunch food you purchased.

This type of lunch packing ends up with lots of hustling about and wasted time which makes it harder for your child to successfully participate in this routine. No wonder if you ask them to help, they forget something. Think how many steps are involved.

Here's how to set up a great system for lunches.

- Rethink your cabinet space. Choose a cabinet to be designated for the lunch center. If you still have short people at your house, be sure to choose a low cabinet so everyone can reach.

- Empty that cabinet of its current stuff. Sort through it and find new homes for those things.
- Gather all of the lunch supplies: Plastic bags of snack and sandwich size, napkins, plastic flatware and all of the non-refrigerated food that you approve of for lunches – even the peanut butter and a loaf of bread and the lunch boxes
- Organize the supplies and the food products in the cabinet.
- For the refrigerated items, use a large plastic container, but remove the lid. Place in it, the lunch meat (make sure it is in its own sealed container), cheese sticks, fruit and so on, that it may be used for lunches. Place it on a shelf next to the drinks purchased for school lunches.
- Take time to instruct the family, pointing out that the lunch cabinet is off limits for after-school snacking. There should be plenty of other things in the pantry for that use. Also point out the section of the fridge that is for packing lunches.
- Packing lunches the evening before is a great way to relieve morning stress. During the after-dinner clean-up, have each child go to the lunch center and choose their side items. The next morning, all that needs to be added is the sandwich and drink. Sandwiches can be made ahead and refrigerated, if you wish.

- Keep the cabinet stocked. Now that everything for lunches is in one spot, it is easy for you to pop open the door and eyeball what is needed from the store.

Keeping Our Goals in Mind

Not too long ago, I was enjoying coffee with a table of professional organizers who all happen to be mothers. We drifted away from the talk of organizing and into the talk of parenting. Pretty soon we began to compare notes and discovered every one of us had something in common. We all had taught our children to be self-sufficient from packing their own lunch to doing their own laundry.

Part of disorganization comes from trying to do everything for everybody. As much as our heart desires us to be that mom who does it all, it simply is not possible or practical. Taking the time to teach your child to be organized is the greatest gift you can give them for they will carry it through their whole life. This includes children packing their book bag and laying out their clothing the night before and packing their own lunch! All you have to do is organize and keep that lunch cabinet stocked. That is enough of a job!

*Mom-to-Mom Tip!

A great tip for stay-at-home moms is to pack their own lunch. When everyone else is packing a lunch, take the time to pack one for yourself and one for your preschooler. Once the kitchen is cleaned up after breakfast, it will stay that way until dinner since you have already dealt with lunch. On a busy day, you will stay healthier, avoiding fast food drive-thrus or all day at-home nibbling. You can quickly grab that lunch to eat at home or take in the car with you on the run. Or, take a moment for a fresh-air picnic with your younger child.

Ideas for Kids and Kitchens

Add a sturdy stepstool to the kitchen. Dragging a chair over isn't only dangerous for the child to stand on but short sighted. You are hoping to teach your child to help often in the kitchen so you should buy a safe stool.

In the kitchen, the organizational lessons, your child learns are many:

Good use of space and keeping like items together: They can learn to organize space by learning the place for everything in the pantry and the cupboards.

Planning ahead: On a larger scale, planning for a week's worth of meals and grocery shopping in advance is a great time saving and a time management technique for you. It is also a lesson in goal setting. In a smaller lesson, preparing a meal or even a recipe is a lesson in organization. You must gather all the items, follow the instructions and pay attention to time needed. You can't bounce around from step one to step four (which certainly some folks try to do when organizing!)

Life skills: Your child might not grow up to be a cook or even to like cooking but hopefully they will. Even so, every adult should have some basic skills. With obesity taking over America, if you don't teach your child to prepare some basic healthy dishes, you are sentencing them to a life of take-out. It isn't only expensive but threatening to weight, heart-health and is linked to cancers, according to articles and news reports.

At the very least, your child should know how to keep a kitchen clean and sanitary and the importance, how to wash produce and some basic skills that will allow them to get by – scramble an egg, make a salad, bake a potato, cook a piece of chicken, boil some pasta and so forth.

Tips for Kids in the Kitchen:

Think safety: Never leave a child alone in a kitchen. Beware of hot stoves, hot oven doors, hot water at the sink, sharp knives, sharp graters, breaking glass and possible falls. Use a sturdy stepstool instead of a chair or placing the child on the countertop. Not only must you be aware, but you must teach the child safety.

Teach sanitation as you go. First kitchen lesson is always to wash your hands before beginning and ending your work in the kitchen. (And possibly in-between if handling animal products- meat, dairy and eggs.)

Take the time to teach organization. Tell the child what you are preparing for the meal. Ask them which task should be done first. This is teaching critical thinking skills and logic. Talk with them about the chores and which one you will do first. For example, explain that since the chicken takes the longest to cook, you must do that one first. We need to take the time to explain things which are all a part of organizing a task.

Choose age appropriate tasks. A young child cannot make a whole salad but they can tear lettuce. Decide what portion of that task they can do. For example, with a step stool, they can stand at the sink and wash the vegetables and rinse the lettuce. They can select the salad dressings from the fridge. You can always find a way for them to participate.

Try these early tasks: Cracking eggs, stirring ingredients, pouring in items, and measuring. There is always something they can help with in any meal.

Recipes for the young: If you are looking for ideas that they can help with from start to finish, try slice and bake cookies, which can be cut with a non-sharp or even plastic knife. Try things made with mixes or fruit smoothies, if you control the blender. You can also offer sandwiches they can build or mixes, dips and spreads which they can eat with veggies or crackers.

Don't expect neatness. Part of the calm in working with a child in the kitchen comes from starting the project with the mindset that it won't be perfectly neat. Fill a sink with warm soapy water for them to drop dirty dishes and spoons into. Place a large cookie sheet with a rim under the bowl they are mixing. It will catch the drips and splatters.

Praise and have fun! Kitchen work can be considered a chore, but why not make it be a fun time with your child? If you sigh and grumble about preparing dinner, they will mimic you and fuss that you are making them "work." But if you concentrate on talking about their day, teaching a bit of organization and cooking, singing along to some fun music, they will have very happy memories of growing up cooking with you. As an adult, they will talk about time with mom in the warmth of that kitchen and the good food and smells they remember. That is the lesson you really want to evoke!

Chapter 17: Organizing Your Fun

Toys, Games, Puzzles and More

There's plenty of family fun to be had – board games, puzzles, video games, computer games, toys and sporting equipment. Use of these items by family members can bring happy times and build memories of a fun home but they can also be a lot of work.

Having a place for everything gives you more time to spend having fun and it teaches your child to be organized. You can't expect them to put their toys and games away when they don't have a home for them.

Here's a round up of ideas for organizing all kinds of fun things.

Ideas for toys:

Banish the toy box: The quaint and old fashioned toy box is just that, out-of-date! Not only are the lids typically dangerous for pinching fingers and slamming down on heads, they actually can pose a danger of strangulation should the lid fall on their neck when they are reaching into the box.

From an organizing point of view, there is nothing worse than a toy box. In a toy box, all the pieces get jumbled together. Little action figures and parts drift to the bottom. To find the parts to play with a toy, the child ends up making a huge mess by digging and dumping everything onto the floor.

If you have a darling toy box that has a safety mechanism on the lid, then you can re-purpose it. Use it as a pillow and blanket chest. Put sleeping bags in it and the extra bedding for the kids get out for sleep-overs or for cuddling into on movie night.

Invest in shelving: From the time you have a baby until that baby gets their own place, shelving will be used. At first, it will hold story books and stuffed animals. Later it will hold toys, books and games. As your child ages, you can add sports trophies, collectables and things related to their hobbies. When they head off to that first apartment, it will go with them to hold books, photos and more. Purchase good quality sturdy shelving as a twenty-five year investment. Be sure to follow safety instructions for bolting it to the wall to prevent it tipping over on children. You can find detailed how-to instructions on the Internet for attaching free-standing shelves to the wall.

Colorful Containers: Larger cars, trucks, dolls and other toys can be lined up on the shelves. Add some plastic containers to keep various parts together. Inexpensive colorful plastic tubs (small ones) or baskets can be found in discount stores for a dollar or two. Use these to sort out blocks, Legos®, action figures, Barbie clothing and so forth. It is worth the organizational effort in order to encourage good imaginary play. It is far too much work for a child to sort through heaps of stuff to find the toys that go together. At that point, their attention span is shot and they are no longer interested.

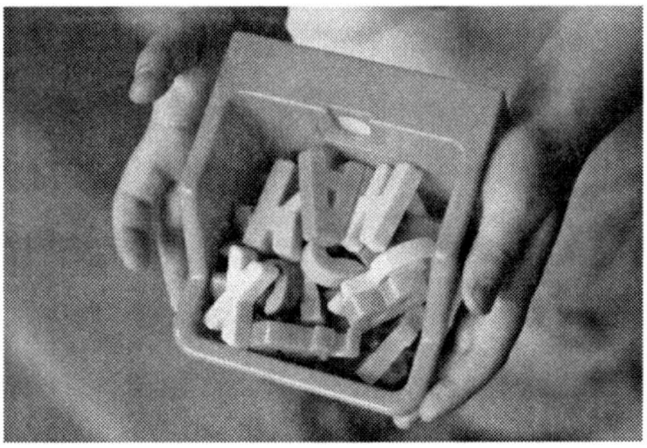

Labels: Help teach organizing by labeling the containers. Remember, we assume that the child understands where the toys belong when we simply say "Put your toys away." Usually that assumption is wrong, as witnessed by the fact that the toys end up in a jumble and you are the one on the floor sorting them out. Grab your digital camera. Shoot some pictures of the container with the toys in it. Print them and use them to label the containers. Or, draw a simple picture of the toy as a label. Now the child, even the non-reader, can easily see which tub has Thomas the Tank Engine® train parts and which has blocks or balls.

Messy Toys: For messy toys, such a puzzles or paints, develop a house rule. Store these items in a high place or a cabinet that the child cannot reach. Items such as puzzles can be "checked out" from the parent, much like checking out a library book. When they bring that puzzle back to you, then they can have another one. For messy toys, from finger paints to bubbles or modeling clay, they can also check them out from you and get your permission to use them when you are available to supervise them at play.

Tub Toys: Sometimes that TMS disease takes over the tub too. That Too-Much-Stuff makes clean-up difficult. Control how many toys are allowed in the tub. If you decide the magic number is 12, then stick to it. If they find a new fun item they want to try in the tub, have them pick something else out of the tub and put it away. There are a number of tub-toy organizers on the market that suction-cup to the wall or hang from the faucet. You can easily

make a tub toy holder out of a plastic container, such as the ones you bought for toys on the shelf. Most of those plastic baskets contain holes on the sides, where water can drain. Use a hammer and a nail or a drill and add a few holes to the bottom of the basket. This will let water that accumulates in the bottom drain out. Set it in the tub, toss in the toys and now you have a tub toy organizer.

***Mom-to-Mom Tip!**

Over time, favorite tub toys can get white with soap scum and look “yucky,” as the kids say. I’ve had success with putting some of them in the top rack of the dishwasher for a good cleaning BUT don’t run the heat dry cycle in case they may melt. Ones that don’t clean up in the dishwasher usually need to go into the trash. If it was that dirty and didn’t clean-up, then we didn’t need it in the tub – or in the baby’s mouth!

Shared Toys: For siblings who are of an age to play together, they may have similar toys. You may have multiples of Bratz™ dolls or Micro cars. The best organizational tip for dealing with these squabbles is to decide on a toy philosophy from the start. One way is to decide that all the toys belong to the household, thus eliminating the “It’s mine” shouting. Or, you can make it a habit to label toys with initials when the children receive the toys. If there is a particular toy that your children squabble over, and it is not feasible to have two of those items, then consider using the odd-even technique. Permanently assign one child to the odd number days of the month and the other child to the even days of the month. The toy is then used by the child on their day, based on the calendar, rather than you daily doling it out by the hour and listening to "It's not fair" speeches.

Board games

It's not especially fun separating the Monopoly money from the Life® money from the Mousetrap® parts.

Board game organization begins with a family rule. Only one board game can be taken out at a time. The first game must be put away neatly before another is taken out.

When preparing to organize board games, ask yourself the same clutter questions you would ask for any project. "Do we love it? Do we use it? Do we need it?" Kids can outgrow a game's age level. The game might be missing parts. The box might have looked fun but the game was boring. Only keep the games you love and use.

Board games are expensive to replace. Make treasured games last longer by storing properly. The biggest mistake in storing games comes from stacking one upon the other until you have a tower of games. The weight of the top games presses on the boxes until you end up with broken and torn boxes, with pieces spilling from the sides and getting lost.

There are a couple of ways to avoid the box-crunching storage.

- Limit your stacks to three games.
- Add additional shelves so that they are closer together and won't hold large stacks.
- Stack the games vertically- think of books on a bookshelf.
- Use an extra dresser to hold board games.
- Use under-the-bed storage boxes to hold board games.

When preparing to organize games, take these additional steps:

1) Reinforce corners of the boxes with clear packing tape.
2) Tape the instructions to the inside of the box. If it is printed on both sides, you can make a copy of the second side.
3) Gather all the pieces and place in a container inside the box. My favorite container is a zippered delicates laundry bag from the $1 store. The mesh bag holds all the pieces and is easy to open and close.
4) Close box with an extra-large rubber band, a Velcro® strip or tie with a ribbon. Store games

each in their own pouch. At a $1 store, you will find drawstring laundry bags in bright colors. Place each game in an individual pouch. It keeps the box, board and pieces together. It makes it easy to carry to family fun nights, game nights or slumber parties. Be sure to label them clearly from the outside

*Mom-to-Mom Tip!

Some game lovers have tackled the amount of storage room games take by ditching the big boxes altogether. To use this organizing technique, tape or glue the instructions on the back of the game board. Place the game pieces in the zippered pouch. Add a hanging tag label to the zipper pull. On your shelf, stack the game boards. Next to that, add a clear plastic container to hold the zippered bags of parts. You will find you can store many, many more games in a small space.

Puzzles

Organize puzzles with these tips.

- For children's wooden puzzles, purchase some clear project envelopes from the office supply store. They usually have a hook and loop closure. You can easily see the puzzle but the pieces are contained. Once they are in the envelopes, they can be stored vertically on a shelf.
- Place jig saw puzzle pieces in a zippered plastic bag.
- Label the bag with the name of the puzzle. If it is difficult to name them, then use numbers. Label the box "Puzzle 3" and the bag of pieces "Puzzle 3."
- Place the bag back in the box or you could cut out the image and put it in the bag and eliminate the box.
- Make a family rule that only one puzzle may be out at a time.

Video games

Don't even think of trying to beat me at Mario Cart or Tetris. Yes, I love video games along with my kids. Of course, those are some old school video games but my point is that I do think video games can be family fun.

What I don't think is fun is the unattractiveness of the game systems. Manufacturers of televisions and entertainment systems have recognized that the items are part of our home's interiors and have adjusted the looks to become more attune to interior design. Video games don't seem to be moving along that line.

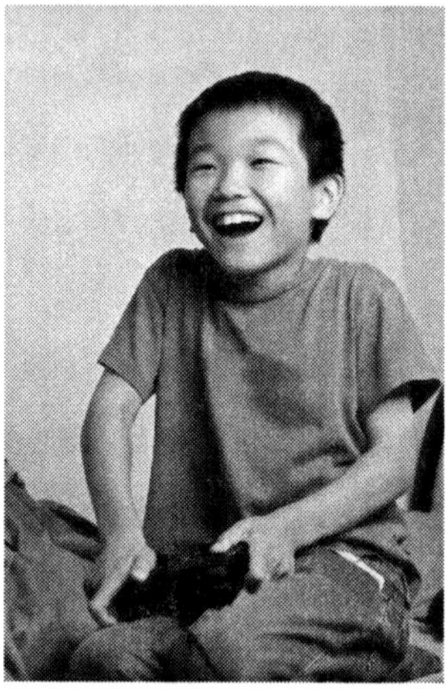

Video games will be a part of your child's world, and maybe yours, forever – or until they leave for college, which feels like forever. You need to make some permanent storage decisions. Find a way to incorporate your game system into the entertainment center or nearby shelving.

A wicker basket can be a great compromise between interior design and having the games available for easy play. Place a wicker basket, even a lidded-one like a picnic basket, near your entertainment center. This will give a place for controls to hide when not in use.

***Mom-to-Mom Tip!**

Another great idea is a controller rack. The Armory Game Controller rack can be mounted into your entertainment system or next to it on the wall. This is a great way to gather up those wired and wireless controllers. You can visit it online at http://www.armorytech.com/

Software-

In organizing home offices for clients, I've filled multiple large trash bags with software boxes. Open a box and typically all that you will find is a CD and a pamphlet. The box is huge and the contents are small. It takes up a ton of storage room.

To organize kid's computer software, purchase a 3-ring binder and a box of clear sheet protectors from the office supply store. There are plenty of fun, kid-themed binders. (By the way, this works just as well for your software!) Place the clear sheet protectors in the binder.

Open each software box. Remove the booklet and paperwork as well as the CD. Place the book and paperwork into the clear sheet protector.

Most, but not all, of the software will have logo artwork on the instruction booklet. This will enable your child to match up the CD with the right sleeve after playing computer games.

If you open a software box and the instructions are not decorated with a logo or artwork, making matching more difficult, you can cut off the face of the box and slip it in the sleeve with the instructions and CD.

Summertime Toys

From boating to river tubing to floating about in the pool, there are plenty of ways for beach bums to make a mess in the summer.

The wet towels, floats, swim vests, goggles and toys are a permanent summer clutter problem.

As with all clutter dilemmas, make a permanent storage decision. Make a splash at organizing by adding two rows of coat hooks to a garage wall or patio wall- one set for each family member and a few for visiting friends. Use the upper hooks for suits and towels.

Use the lower hooks for vests and goggles. Add a plastic laundry basket below each set for the water toys and swim shoes.

If you have rafts or water noodles, add two metal hooks to the wall. Use a bungee cord, hooked to each hook, to hold the floats upright.

Final chore: Label! Add each person's name above their hook and the water goodies are under control.

***Mom-to-Mom Tip!**

During the winter, these hooks can hold jackets or bags for that season's sports equipment or snow play.

Garage: Outdoor Toys and Sports Equipment

Many garages contain a pegboard for organizing tools. This inexpensive organizer also works will with kids' gear. You may want to mount one lower than you would for adults. Pegs on the board can hold baseball gloves, ball caps, shin guards, helmets of all kinds, tennis rackets and so forth. Cleats and other special shoes can hang from hooks too.

Square or rectangular plastic baskets can be attached to the pegboard with a couple of hooks. These baskets can hold tennis balls, golf balls, batting gloves and all manner of small sporting gear.

You can also organize sports equipment for family members using the previous idea for swimming gear. If a pegboard isn't feasible, purchase some coat hooks from the home improvement store. You can get them for less than $2. Line several up vertically for each athlete in the family.

Attach a basket to one to hold balls and other small items. Caps, mitts, shin guards, helmets and so forth can go on the hooks. Purchase some inexpensive frames for about $2 each and place an extra sports photo of the child above his hook. It will label the gear as his and turn that garage into a personalized locker room.

Sports fanatics always seem to have a lot of tall pieces that simply won't hook on a pegboard. These range from putters to ball bats to hockey sticks. A large, tall trash can is great help for holding these items. Place a few bricks or other heavy item in the bottom to keep it from tipping over.

***Mom-to-Mom Tip!**

Need a fast, cheap way to organize sports equipment for multiple kids? Purchase a number of tall kitchen trash cans, around $4-$5 each. Place the children's names on each. Line them up in the garage and let them use them to keep up with their gear. It is not quite as efficient as being able to see everything, such as on a pegboard, but it can get the job done in a hurry.

Chapter 18: Organizing for Safety

Being Ready for Disaster

In the dark of the night, my heart would start pounding like a drum. In the distance, the wail of the tornado siren was just loud enough to filter through my dreams and start the adrenaline rushing. In 2004, my then hometown of Jackson, Tennessee lost 22 people to an F-4 level tornado. In fact, it was the third tornado experienced in a short time in that area. I'd race down the hall, every time the siren sounded, tugging sleeping kids from their beds and force their grumbling persons to the basement.

Now a Florida resident, my new friends and neighbors share tales of their loss in Hurricanes Ivan and Dennis. Two of my friends lost their entire homes to the sea. Out in California, fires rage and earthquakes awake residents. Up north, my friends in the cold bunker down against deep snow and ice storms.

Organizing with and for children means you should be taking into consideration safety issues. It most certainly is an important part of household organization.

Take the time to learn the details of safety disasters that may strike your region of the country. For each disaster, I have included an expert disaster website for more information. My goal for including this in the book is to remind you of the importance of organizing and preparing for disasters. It is important to keep our priorities straight. It is great to want more organization, less clutter and neater kids' rooms but first and foremost we must always do what we need to keep our families safe.

Key Safety Essentials to Teach Children

Teach all children how and when to call 9-1-1, police, or the fire department.

Teach children their whole name, parents' names, address and phone #.

Teach children to respond to and listen for dangerous weather alerts on the weather radio.

Teach children, who are old enough to be home alone, how to find the local radio station in order to tune in for current emergency information.

Create an emergency center - a drawer or cabinet. Place in it flashlights, extra batteries, a transistor radio and copies of emergency phone numbers they might need.

Make sure at least one phone in your house works without electricity.

Fire Safety Organization:

No matter where you live, everyone needs to organize for fire safety.

- Have a fire escape plan. Every plan should have two exits. If you go to the first exit and it is blocked, you should have an alternate way out.
- Discuss the fire escape plan with your children. Have a fire drill. Practice using both exits. Pretend one is blocked. Make sure they know how to unlock and open windows.
- Practice fire safety tips. Such as: feeling doors to see if they are hot; crawling to stay under the smoke; and stop, drop and roll if encountering a flame on you. Learn more about fire safety at http://www.usfa.dhs.gov/kids/parents-teachers/lesson_plan.shtm.
- Have a meeting point. You don't want to be racing around trying to find each other. You might use the mailbox for a meeting point. It is away from the house and fire. It is a focal point everyone can find.
- You can place signs or stickers in bedroom windows that alert firefighters of the presence of babies or pets that need assistance.

Organizing for Tornado Safety:

Almost all parts of the country can experience possible tornado weather. Have a tornado weather plan. If you have children old enough to stay home by themselves on occasion, then they are old enough to be aware of tornado safety precautions. They should know where to go to be safe.

Purchase a weather radio. If your community does not have sirens, and many do not, then the weather radio will sound an alarm when you are in danger from a tornado.

Choose a safe place. The safest spots are the lowest levels of your home. If you have a basement, go there. If not, go to the ground floor. Choose a location on the ground floor that does not have any windows, such as a hallway, bathroom or closet. If possible, choose one in the center of the house and one that doesn't have any exterior walls.

Visit FEMA for more info at http://www.fema.gov/news/newsrelease.fema?id=2920.

Organizing for a Hurricane:

There are many steps to preparing for a hurricane. One of the best resources for this is at the National Hurricane Center website at http://www.nhc.noaa.gov/HAW2/english/disaster_prevention.shtml. At this site, you will find information and lists to help you prepare your family and your children to be ready for an approaching hurricane.

Prepare some checklists for your family so that you know what you will be packing in the event of an evacuation to either a safer location or to a shelter. In organizing for children, pack a backpack of games and activities as well as a comforting and familiar doll, stuffed animal or blanket.

Be sure to consider babies, children and teens special needs in your packing list. Do you need prescription or over-the-counter medications? Diapers and formula? Special foods?

Part of being prepared is learning the steps involved. Let your children help to check off the list and help prepare the family. They are learning to be organized for safety and it makes them feel good to help you.

Organizing for Earthquakes:

Turn to the Red Cross for a great list for help in organizing your family for an earthquake. You can visit http://www.redcross.org/services/disaster/0,1082,0_583_,0 0.html.

You really must work on organizing for an earthquake with your child as it will happen without warning. Practice choosing a safe location in each room of the house with earthquake drills. Check the Red Cross website for a better understanding of safe locations in your home- away from windows and heavy falling furniture, like bookcases.

Practice drop, cover and hold-on with your children.

This Red Cross website contains special materials for teaching children how to be prepared for an earthquake, including a coloring book that you can download.

Organizing for Ice or Snow Storms:

The NorthStar Preparedness Network can help you prepare your family for winter weather, which can be lethal. Turn to http://www.preparednessnetwork.org/northstar/seasonal/snow.html. You will find checklists for preparing your home and car for this weather.

Chapter 19: Labeling

Organize with Labels

Oh the Drama!

Oh woe is me, cries the child, throwing their arm dramatically across their eyes.

Actually, the cry is more like "Mom, he took my box of crayons" or "Mom, where are the craft paints."

No matter what the disorganization drama of the moment, it might have been solved with a label.

After days of hunting for an important document, I had a man turned to me for help with his paperwork. There were stacks and stacks of manila folders and each contained a particular subject and none of them were labeled. Like magic, I found his missing document (Alright, so it took a couple of hours but he thought it was magic). And then I asked him, "Why is this folder blank? If it was so important, why does it not have a label?"

"Because if write on it, I can't use it again," he said.

Four cents. Four cents. They cost four cents each! How much is your time worth? How much time do you spend hunting for stuff that you could have found right away with a label?

Remember that dresser earlier in the book, the one with every drawer overstuffed with every manner of clothing.

Part of the cure for that problem is labels. Both adults and children respond to labels and they don't at all respond to assumptions.

You can assume all you want that your child can see socks in the top drawer so they surely know that socks go in the top drawer. As our good friend Dr. Phil says, "How is that working for you?"

Label. Label. Label.

Think how much you would enjoy NOT being the household index. What if people didn't have to constantly ask you where things were? What if they opened the cabinets and could find things for themselves? Organization and self-responsibility are not separable.

Chapter 20: Ready Set Go!

How to Implement the Ideas in This Book

I know what you're thinking!

It's most likely a mixture of excitement, anxiety and determination.

You are excited to think about the possibility that ***"Your child, no matter if toddler or teen, can learn to be more personally responsible and organized."***

It is exciting to think how it might take some of the burden off of you, making you a more cheerful and fun parent instead of a stressed out one. For the parent of little ones, you should now have some good ideas of things to teach your child and steps to work on as they age.

For the parent of an older child, you are probably wishing you had started this when they were two years old. Now you wonder if it is too late. You are filled with a certain amount of anxiety. While you can see the potential benefits of teaching your child to be organized, you wonder if you have enough stamina to deal with the battle. After all, if someone had been waiting on us hand and foot, as the saying goes, would we want to do the work ourselves? You might even be wondering if it would be easier to just do it all yourself and forget the whole idea.

Underneath the excitement and anxiety lies determination. You are determined to improve things in your home and to not always be setting yourself up to be the bad guy.

All of those feelings are normal. Think about this, aren't those the very same feelings you have about any organizing project? Aren't you excited to envision the finished project, anxious about getting it done and determined to make changes? Teaching your child to be organized is one big organizing project.

At the beginning of this book, I shared some truths with you. They were:

You can get rid of clutter.

You can become organized.

Your children can learn personal responsibility for their things.

The family can work together.

Your children can learn to care for their room, do their laundry, assist around the house, and manage their time and more. What they can't do is tackle all of those things at the same time! Imagine if I told you that you were going to make so many changes at one time. It would be far too stressful.

The parents of very young children can gradually begin to implement organizing into their daily routine. You can clap and encourage them to drop their clothes in the hamper. You can add labels to toy baskets. You can rearrange the kitchen cabinets so they can reach their own dishes. As you go through each chapter, you will find ideas for things young children can accomplish. They can grow up learning to be organized.

For older children and teens, there will most likely be a number of things to work on. As a parent, you need to decide which organizing project will be most beneficial to your child. For one parent, they may have read this book and realized that part of the struggle at home is the lack of set time and place for homework and thus there is a daily battle. For another, they may feel like every morning is chaos and realize that a launch pad is the place to begin.

Here's how to get started:

1) **Grab a notebook or folder for keeping your organizing notes**. You will want to be able to keep and refer back to these lists.

2) **Make an actual written list of the things you wish were more organized in your child's life.** Here are a few ideas:

- Getting out the door in the morning
- Homework and evening routines
- Piles of school papers
- Laundry
- Clutter in every room
- Child's room is in chaos
- Can't get themselves ready, or on time, in the morning
- Preparing meals and kitchen is crazy
- Family chores
- Always losing things
- Always running late

1) **Priorities can change.** For now, choose the top two things to work on. You might be choosing them because the child is upset (battling over homework times) or because you are upset (being the constant reminder service or the only one performing chores for the whole family.) After you have tackled the top three, then you can pull out this list and reevaluate and choose two more.

2) **Create a list for the top two items.**

You will list each thing that must happen in order for your child to be more organized in that area. For example, if you wish your child to have a more organized room, what needs to happen next? Do you need to have an organizing appointment with your child and follow the steps in this book? Do you need to purge out old toys and clothes? Do you need shelves or other organizing products? Do you need family rules to keep it that way? Make a list of each thing that needs to happen for your goal to be finished.

3) **Sit down with your child and talk about organizing that space or a new way of doing things**, such as a new morning routine. Remember, you are teaching them to be organized. Take the time to listen to their ideas and complaints. Tell them that organizing means trying new things. If the old way was working well, you wouldn't be looking for a new way. If the new way doesn't work, then you will both try something else. Ask them to give the new way a chance first, before fussing. Pull out the calendar and together choose a time to do some organizing.

4) **Break working with an older child into stages,** especially if want them to take over chores you formerly did, break it into stages. Give them a time frame and a goal. For example, you might say something like "By spring break, I'm going to expect you to be able to do your own laundry (or help with laundry- depending on their age.) Don't announce "From this day forward, you are doing your own laundry." Remember, you are teaching them to be more organized. On your calendar, break down the steps. First couple of weeks, they may help gather and sort laundry and you work with them on time management. Work on how they will fit laundry into their schedule. Next few weeks, they may start the washer and dryer. Then next couple weeks, they add folding- all the while you are supervising. Over the course of a month or two, you walk them through all the steps.

5) **Don't start another lesson until you are satisfied with the first one.** Once you have taken the time to work your way through all the steps in a task, and they seem to have the routine down, then you can go on to the next organizing lesson you wish to work on. Remember, you will need to be reminding them to

check their chore list or homework list. As a parent, it is still your responsibility to see that things are done but it is not your responsibility to do them all yourself.

6) **Encourage and reward**. Thank your child for completing their organizing task. Encourage your child for their efforts. Find ways to reward your child. As your child or teen takes on more of their own organizing, demonstrate how that free time benefits the family. Take the time to read an extra story one night while telling them "I have time to read this extra story because you emptied the dishwasher. Thank you for helping to keep the house organized by doing your chores." Or, bake some cookies or have family card game, telling your teens that you have time to do more fun family things because they are being more responsible for themselves.

7) **Gentle reminders go a long way**. Sure they are going to forget. We adults also forget things. A cheerful reminder or well-placed sticky note can often do the trick.

8) **Be prepared for the time monster to appear**. When you have an expectation that your child is to do a chore or organize for themselves, but they did not, be prepared for the

time monster. This is when they say that they don't have time to pick-up their room or lay out their clothes or whatever the task may be. Sometimes, kids are truly over burdened. Other times, they are simply not interested in the task at hand. When the time monster appears, go over their schedule for the rest of the day or the next day and see if you can suggest a way to fit it in their day. Instead of offering to do it for them, offer to let it slide until the next day when they can do it. When they really get into a bind, do offer to help them out. Remind them that one very busy day, you will expect the favor to be returned when you need help.

As parents, we need to walk a fine line here. We don't want them to think that parents are here to do their every wish or that they must handle all tasks alone. On the other hand, we do want them to know that family members pitch in and stick up for each other.

9) **Be positive and focused, but, also be prepared with consequences.** It is great to work hard at getting them to contribute to organizing. Hopefully, it can be done with cheerful encouragement, high expectations, praise and rewards. On the other hand, I'm a mom and I know that doesn't always work. Think ahead of the consequences. Always remember that it is your job

to do a good job teaching and supervising. Once the child has mastered the task then expect them to continue to perform it. Remind them. Encourage them. When they are capable of doing the task but just did not do it, either refusing or simply wasting their time away, then be prepared to be firm and issue consequences.

*Mom-to-Mom Tip!

Best rule of thumb for time management with a child: ***Don't always give in*** and do it for them because they ran out of time. ***Don't always be stubborn*** and never help them out. Your first goal is to try to help them see a way to accomplish the task themselves.

Key Tips to Keep in Mind

- Make a written plan.
- Keep a notebook.
- Use your calendar to spread out tasks you want to work on.
- Break things into smaller jobs when needed.
- Daily – remember they are going to model themselves after what you do and not what you say. Have a plan to work on your own organizing skills and projects.
- If it doesn't work, change it. Don't fail to change.

You know how you vow to get organized one of these days?

Make today the day.

Chapter 21 Worksheet

Organize Right Now

Growing-Up Organized: Mom -to-Mom Tips©

By Professional Organizer Lea Schneider

Worksheet: Deciding Where to Begin

Ranking: 1= organized, 5 = quite disorganized	1	2	3	4	5
Bedroom: How would you describe your child's bedroom on a typical day?					
Closet: Can they find what they need in the closet? Is it user friendly? Is the storage in it well used or filled with junk?					
Clothing: Jackets and clean clothing hung up. Dirty clothing in hamper? Able to find socks and pairs of shoes?					
Staying Tidy: After a big "clean-sweep" in your child's room, does it stay tidy or return to chaos quickly?					
Clutter: Does your child contribute to family clutter—leaving things here and there in the house for someone else to deal with?					
Chores: Does your child view chores as a family responsibility? Do they understand chores are their responsibility for their time & space?					
Homework: Does disorganization on when and where to do homework create daily struggles?					
Paperwork: Is there a home for kids' paperwork or is it here, there and everywhere?					

Continued

Ranking: 1= organized, 5 = quite disorganized	1	2	3	4	5
Paperwork: Does your child have a home for school/art papers and responsibility to file them away or is that left up to you?					
Memory: Are you constantly reminding your child of everything from permission slips to soccer cleats or to brush their teeth?					
Toys & Games: Do toys, games and sports gear have a home? Does your child take care to put toys away nicely?					
Laundry: How organized is your child with laundry? Can they perform age appropriate laundry tasks?					
Kitchen Capers: Can your child perform age appropriate kitchen tasks– either making food or cleaning up or helping you?					
Leaving for School: Does a lack of a morning routine make your family a crazy one in the morning?					
Time Management: Does your child know where to be when, if homework is due and can juggle chores, school and activities?					
Safety: Do you have a safety plan for disasters? Have you reviewed it with your child– in an age appropriate way?					
Responsibility: When you assign your child a task or chore, can you count on it being done or do they forget or make excuses?					

Review your child's scores and move on to the next section, keeping your scores in mind.

Finding a Focus

The previous page's written rankings should give you an indication of what kinds of organizing might benefit you and your child. Clearly anything that scored a 4 or 5 should be given high priority. There is always room for improvement in areas scoring a 3 or 4. Concentrate on the 4 and 5 scores but don't be afraid to implement ideas that might help in areas of 3 or 4.

Suppose you have LOTS of 4's and 5's? You might even have all 4's or 5's. You should only begin to work on one area at a time. How do you choose which one to begin with?

Time Deadlines

Do any of these have a deadline? For example, your child might be having a poor term in school and you want to focus on homework disorganization in order to start to turn things around as soon as possible. A stay-at-home mom might be returning to the workforce and feel that she needs to get that morning routine organized ASAP.

Look to see if any of your 4's or 5's that have a time deadline. If there isn't a time deadline, then move on to the next question. Project with a time deadline:____________________________________

Emotional deadlines

Do any of these issues cause frustration? Perhaps emotional outbursts or upset? (That could be either parent or child!) For example: Is there a constant fight over the state of the bedroom? Does the quantity of laundry almost drive you to tears?

Look to see if any of the 4's or 5's cause someone else to be upset. Circle the issue that <u>first</u> comes to mind as the most frustrating. Number the rest 2, 3, 4 etc so you will know your next projects.

Focus

You should now have a good idea of where to begin. If you have an organizational issue that has a time deadline, you must work on that first, even if there are more frustrating issues. If you have more than one time-deadline issue, then choose the one that appears to be of most importance.

If you haven't any time deadlines, then you will move on to the emotional issue that you chose on the previous page.

Organizing Issue To Work on ________________________________

Child's Input

Never, ever spring an organizing project on your child. The more you work together, the more cooperation you can hope for. For the very youngest, it is enough to be happy and positive. Demonstrate the organizing tasks. Get them to be your helper and praise them as you go. They don't need to know there is a "plan" as long as you have goals in mind.

For the older child, once you have some clear goals in your mind, sit down with your child and talk about the organizing issues in a positive voice. For example "I see you are frustrated with getting homework done. I don't want you to be unhappy. Let's work on a new plan for how we tackle homework." Or, "I feel sad when you and I get in a tug-of-war over the state of your room. I'd like to work with you to come up with a plan that will satisfy both of us."

For older children and teens, having a voice and opinion is important. Offer organizing choices you can live with. For example, you might sit down and talk about coming up with better routines and being more organized and that you want a more peaceful house. You might point out two areas you'd like to help them work on and tell them why.

Ask them which one they'd like to focus on first. Consider their input and suggestions and take those suggestions whenever possible. Remember that the goal is for them to accept responsibility for been being more organized. The first step toward that is having them accept some of the responsibility for choosing the project.

After talking with your child and listening to their point of view, do you still have the same project?

What is the first project:

____

Goal Setting

Take the time to come up with a written goal. You must have a clear idea of what your are working toward. Make sure your older children participate in setting the goal and other steps, under your supervision.

For example, if morning time management is your issue, your goal might be: For the child to be ready in the morning for the bus or car-pool on time. This includes dressed, breakfast eaten, face washed, teeth brushed, hair combed, coat/gloves or other outerwear on, book bag packed, lunch in hand and so forth.

Another example might be bedroom organization: Your goal might be for a neat, organized room with a place for everything and a written plan for how it will be kept organized.

Goal: At the end of this project, we want:

____

Breaking Down the Task

Every organizing project contains multiple tasks. For example, if you want to get out the door in the morning, you might need to rearrange things and come up with a launch pad. You might need to buy baskets and hooks. You might need wipe-off boards and new rules for the morning routine.

An organizing bedroom project will have a number of steps. You might need to sort and clear the clutter and old toys. See if you need any organizing products. Come up with a new room arrangement or storage for things. Clean the room. Organize the space. Add labels. Write rules for keeping it organized. Start a new routine for how it will be kept.

Think of all the steps in your project. Don't worry about listing them in order now. Just write down everything that comes to mind for this task. You can always add to it later. Refer to the chapter of this book that offers idea for your chosen area. *Once you have listed everything, then number the tasks in the order they need to be done.*

Jot down any reminders or ideas that come to you while working on this list.

Task List Continued on next page….

Task List

____

____

____

____

____

____

____

____

Gathering Supplies

There is nothing more frustrating and time wasting than starting something and stopping to go to the store. List here the products or supplies you need for this job. For example, trash bags, boxes, markers, tape, labels, file folders, coat hooks and so on.

*Note! Don't buy organizing products, such as tubs or bins, until you have purged out the clutter. You may not need as many as you thought or you may need bigger ones or smaller ones. Don't buy any organizing products until you have a plan in mind for the space. You have to know WHERE you are going to put items before you can decide HOW you are going to store them.

List all supplies you need to start the job. Purchase organizing products later.

Supply List:

Reward Yourself

Make this be a good time for you and your child. Plan a reward for the finished project. Watch a movie together. Read a story. Build an ice-cream sundae. Play the board game of their choosing.

You may need to have multiple organizing sessions or projects. What are some of the different kinds of reward you can plan on having.

____

____

____

____

What is the first reward for the first project?

Planning

Grab your calendar (and your child if they are old enough to help you plan the project. Remember, planning and pacing projects is a time management lesson.) Look at the steps you listed for your project. Find opportunities on your calendar to tackle each of the steps. Don't choose an all-day organizing event as even a teen doesn't have that kind of attention span. You'd only be tired and frustrated by the second half of the day. If you have a big project, try a half-day Saturday and a half-day Sunday. Or, break it into smaller chunks. You can always break a room into zones, or walls, doing one wall each appointment.

List your appointments here. Be write them on your calendar. If something interferes with your plan, be sure to pick another date.

<u>Appointments to Organize</u>:

At the end of each Organizing Session

For physical organizing: Take trash outside. Place donation items in car. Label anything in stacks– such as "sort thru this" or "give to neighbor" so that you can remember what the stacks are for.

For organizing time or other issues: Have your child repeat back to you how the organizing will work, in order to make sure they understand the new plan. Make yourself reminder notes so that you can help the child establish a new routine or way of doing things.

Go over plans for next appointment. What task will be worked on and when?

Praise and hug your child or teen. Always end on a happy note.

If this is the end of that project, except for maintenance, then make sure that you and they have agreed how this area or way will be maintained. Don't forget the promised reward.

Discuss what organizing item will be tackled next.

Donation agency or location:

What kind of reminders are needed?

Is there a way for the child to remind themselves?

What last minute tasks or products are needed to finish the job?

Additional Notes:

Chapter 23

Growing-Up Organized: Mom -to- Mom Tips©

By Professional Organizer Lea Schneider

Resources: Books to Teach Organizing

Parents can get their child involved in stories that involve clutter or being messy. These stories allow children to imagine what kinds of things happen when disorganization rules the house.

They provide a great way for you to open up dialog and talk about making organizing plans and rules for your own house and for their room.

Fritz and the Mess Fairy

This book, by Rosemary Wells, is a paper book by Picture Puffins. It is out-of-print but available through on-line used books stores. Simply enter the title in your search engine.

In this story, a young skunk gets in trouble by stuffing a month's worth of laundry, dirty dishes, spoons and piles of old Halloween candy under his bed. Chaos, clutter and consequences, all with a humorous twist, teach lessons to 4 to 8 year olds.

The Berenstain Bears Think of Those in Need

This paperback, by Stan and Jan Berenstain is available both new and used on-line or purchase or order at a book-store. The publisher is First Time Books.

The Bear Family has too much stuff– everywhere! It is stuffed in closets and drawers! Mama Bear teaches the family to clear out the clutter of old toys, books and games while helping those in need by donating to a store that helps the children's hospital.

My Messy Room

This book by Jessica Steinbrenner is a paperback that tells the story of Robert. Robert needs to clean his room but is so do distracted by his roomful of toys

Organize Right Now

Resources: Websites

T

he following website are great if you would like to find more advice or perhaps participate in discussion forums.

Get Organized Now– Look for the forums link.
http://www.getorganizednow.com/

Online Organizing

http://www.onlineorganizing.com/ExpertAdvice.asp

Fly Lady- Self Help in Organizing

http://www.flylady.com/

Find Your Own Professional Organizer

http://www.napo.net/

You will always find tips and seasonal advice
at the
Organize Right Now site.

www.organizerightnow.com

The Berenstain Bears and the Messy Room

In this Stan and Jan Berenstain book, Mama Bear is always cleaning the children's' room. She gets worn out. She threatens to throw away the messy toys but instead the whole family pitches in and organizes the room.

Mark's Messy Room

Author Geraldine Elschner brings readers the story of Carlo the cat in this hardback. Poor Carlo has to live in Mark's messy bedroom. Carlo leaves to find a neat house but learns about missing his friend, Mark.

Resources: Shopping

The Container Store

http://www.containerstore.com/

Home Depot

www.homedepot.com

Mister Plexi– Clear Organizing Products

www.misterplexi.com

Stacks and Stacks Homewards

http://www.stacksandstacks.com/

Ikea
http://www.ikea.com/us/en/

Organize
http://www.organize.com/

Solutions
http://www.solutions.com/jump.jsp?itemID=0&itemType=HOME_PAGE

Target
http://www.target.com/gp/homepage.html/602-9345994-9160610?node=1038576

Get Organized Spacesavers
http://www.shopgetorganized.com/prodetail.asp?src=GOOG0305&itemno=22996

Resources: Other Helpers

Meal Planning Help

http://www.heb.com/mealtime/MP-lastWeek.jsp
http://www.crockpot.com/

Garage Sale tips

http://www.ifg-inc.com/Consumer_Reports/GarageSale.shtml

Keeping Tax Records for donated Items

http://www.ehow.com/how_13129_keep-proper-records.html

Reminder Services

http://www.free-minder.com/

Friends and Family

Don't forget that friends and family make great resources. Turn to parents who you admire and ask them for tips.

Pay attention to techniques that you see friends use to stay organized. They'll enjoy the compliment. Just like you might enjoy sharing a recipe, a favorite paperback or a movie you watched, you can enjoy sharing organizing ideas with one another.

Chapter 24 Sorting Labels

Labels for Organizing

The following pages contain printable signs for working on organizing your child's room.

Organize Right Now

Garage Sale

www.organizerightnow.com

Organize Right Now

Trash

www.organizerightnow.com

Organize Right Now

Put in New spot

www.organizerightnow.com

Organize Right Now

Sort This

www.organizerightnow.com

Organize Right Now

Donate

www.organizerightnow.com

Organize Right Now

Keep

www.organizerightnow.com

Cover Art Credits:
Soccer Ball ©jberg-fotolia.com,Yield ©Harris Shiffman-fotolia.com
9 o'clock alarm clock© Niklaw Ramberg-fotolia.com, Rattle© Juliya Shumskaya-fotolia.com, Spelling Grade© Graca Victoria-fotolia.com, Cheque with Pen© Feng Ya-fotolia.com, Rubber Duckling© Emin Ozkan-fotolia.com, Red female shoes© terex School bus back© hanzi-fotolia.com, Red peg (hanger) ©Aleksandr Ugorenkov-fotolia.com, Grocery bag ©Edyta Pawlowska-fotolia.com, Baking Ingredients ©Graca Victoria-fotolia.com, Socks and underwear in basket© Dori O'Connell-fotolia.com, and Blue Sponge© Robert Cocquyt-fotolia.com.

Inside Art Credits:
Girls standing face to face© iofoto-fotolia.com, Asian kid playing game© Jamie Choy-fotolia.com, Making cookies 008 ©Tom Perkins-fotolia.com, Big pile of books ©Juliam Rovagnati-fotolia.com, Boy student ©Tom Perkins-fotolia.com, School supplies on yellow background ©Michael Filppo-fotolia.com, Girl with dresses (luggage)© Hallgerd-fotolia.com, School lunch ©Graca Victoria-fotolia.com, Baby clothes ©Andres Rodriquez-fotolia.com, Boys with beach towels ©Sonya Etchison-fotolia.com, To do list ©Graca Victoria-fotolia.com, Baby lying down© Eric Isselee-fotolia.com, Going crazy ©Laurin Rinder-fotolia.com, Washing the dishes© Hallgerd-fotolia.com, Pretty woman vacuuming© Stephen Coburn-fotolia.com, Teenager mowing the lawn ©Ken Hurst-fotolia.com, Toys ©Marzana Syncerz-fotolia.com, Hanging bath toys ©Joseph Paolineui-fotolia.com, Children play with pillows© Pavel Losevsky-fotolia.com
Storage containers ©Scott Rothstein-fotolia.com, Back to school – boy with backpack ©senicphoto-fotolia.com, Doing household chores© Tracy Martinez-fotolia.com, and Sunny child's room© Hallgerd-fotolia.com., puppy with red scarf © Anyka-fotolia.com, baby crawling on white background studio shoot © Slobodan Vasic-fotolia.com, heart in hand © Andreas Gradin-fotolia.com, storage containers © Scott Rothstein-fotolia.com

About the Author

Professional Organizer Lea Schneider and her team at Organize Right Now help people from all over to organize. With their Organize Online program, using phone and email, you can get expert advice and a plan for everything from piles of papers to walk-in closets missing their floors.

Her organizing advice has appeared in *Woman's Day, Natural Health, Better Homes and Gardens Kids' Rooms* magazines, websites such as *My Roommate is Driving Me Crazy* and *What's Cooking America.*

She is the Grand Prize Winner of the Rolodex Office Makeover Challenge. She is a discussion moderator for professional organizers from all over the world at Get Organized Now.com.

As a working mother of three, she developed time management and household organizing ideas. As a feature reporter for daily newspapers, she wrote about issues relating to home, family, gardening and food. A freelance writer, she is a member of the Association of Food Journalists and is a member of the National Association of Professional Organizers

Her favorite Mom must-haves: a paper planner, coffee and chocolate, a sense of humor and five minutes of me-time daily!

Contact the Author: Contact her through her website at www.organizerightnow.com.

2547730

Made in the USA